I Just Had To Get On With It

George Ellis Parkinson

authorHOUSE®

AuthorHouse™ UK Ltd.
500 Avebury Boulevard
Central Milton Keynes, MK9 2BE
www.authorhouse.co.uk
Phone: 08001974150

©2011 George Ellis Parkinson. All rights reserved.

No part of this book may be reproduced, stored in a retrieval system, or transmitted by any means without the written permission of the author.

First published by AuthorHouse   10/6/2011.

ISBN: 978-1-4567-7273-4 (sc)

Any people depicted in stock imagery provided by Thinkstock are models, and such images are being used for illustrative purposes only.
Certain stock imagery © Thinkstock.

This book is printed on acid-free paper.

Because of the dynamic nature of the Internet, any Web addresses or links contained in this book may have changed since publication and may no longer be valid. The views expressed in this work are solely those of the author and do not necessarily reflect the views of the publisher, and the publisher hereby disclaims any responsibility for them.

This story is dedicated to my cousin Raymond, who suggested that I must put onto paper (I have cursed him a time or two when my fingers wont obey my thoughts).

Also many thanks to my Private Secretary, my Great Granddaughter Ellen, without her expertise my ramblings would still be on my Lap Top.

Forword

If l lapse into my native dialect you will have to forgive me, You see I have had quite a few years to perfect it. If you can not understand some of my expressions you will have to go to W H Smith.s and purchase a sixpenny booklet. A year or two ago I purchased (how to be a secretary/how to be a Chairman) so they should have on sale now, how to understand a Yorkie.

I will try to illustrate, when coming out of mine one day in the paddy train., a rather thick set Polish chap was taking up three seats, I said to him, '' Square thi sen round". He loked at me like a piece of tripe,.so I said to him "What's up, can't tha understand plain english"...I could not understand why he didn't. After on of my tests, during my juggling with Jesus times, I was told I would have done better if I had been able to express myself more clearly. I hope I have improved.

The time has come me cousin said
To write of many things.
Of trains and planes and coal mines.
And many other things.
Trials and temptations I have had my fill.
But time comes by to pay the bill.
I hope this tale you will enjoy,
I know that some it will annoy.
Of ups and downs I have had my share,
But who was it said that life was fair.
I will leave you with this little note.
It should fill you with some hope
Today was tomorrow yesterday.
Let's hope it will forever stay.

With apologies to Lewis Carroll and friends)

I am now in my eightieth eighth year and I have two things that I really do regret, I wish that I had put my story to paper years ago when the grey matter was a bit more active and my memory would have been much better. My other failing is I wish I had taken more photographs.

My earliest recollection is looking into a field and seeing a lot of Pheasants. It must have been in early September they were obviously pecking at the remnants of the harvest. I would have been almost four years old.

We lived in the village of Kexborough Nr Barnsley, in the middle of the coal mining district. Our address was Balls Row Church field Lane, it was a back to back terrace of eight houses, four one bed roomed houses and two bed roomed houses. At the back was Wilfred Allot and his Wife, Mrs Speight and one daughter, Fred Allot his wife and eight children, Mr and Mr Milton Beaumont and his wife, who was totally blind, she was born without eyes, but she would never admit it. Whenever I had some new clothing I had to go round and *show* them to her, always she would say my word Georgia you do look smart! It was said she once had a milliners shop HOW? Milton was the Sunday School Superintendent, he was a hypocrite, he treated his wife very badly, she once left him and walked back to the village where she was born, a distance of five miles. At the front were Charles and Annie Ellis my grandparents, and nine children. Then Henry and Mary Allot and seven children Wilfred Alfred Jarvis Violet Mary Kenneth, and Joyce (Joyce was quite a girl) she taught me more than the rudiments about the birds and bees.

Next was my parents Walter and Ethel Parkinson I had one sister Doreen who was one year and a day older than me. Next were Walter and Emma Hawksworth and her sister Miss Horbury these houses were one up and one down and two up and two down, I think some of the children were hung up on clothing hooks to sleep at night.

Miss Horbury was a very staunch Salvationist she had spent most of her life in the east end of London (when that part of London was a very rough place),she was a very good *religious* person and did a lot of good in Darton West where in late twenties and thirties unemployment was practically normal. To me, this 'depression' is a flea bite compared to those days. As I said she was very religious person, on a Sunday she would walk six miles to the nearest Citadel and of course walk back. Alas on the last occasion she got knocked down by a bus (that she refused to ride on) and was killed, what a sad end to a wonderful life. Quite often my dad and I would go next door to play at Ludo, all the time we were playing she would be Tut Tutting.

Grandmas, Allots and Beaumont's were two up and two down, these fortunate people had the luxury of four rooms to raise there families. We all had the same facilities gas lighting, one gas ring. Running water (some of the time) we all had water butts to catch the rain water. We sometimes had to go with a ladling can to be able to wash.

We had a Yorkshire Range coal burning fireplace, with a side boiler that had be filled and emptied with a lading can, at the other side was an oven. Which had to cleaned every week with a coal rack and if it got really bad we used to put a spewer in (that's a small firework). Its purpose was to clear all the nooks and crannies. The flooring was flag stones which were covered with oilcloth, if you were posh linoleum. Rag rugs were made on a frame with Hessian sacks and old clothes.

We all had large callers where the coal was kept, Grandmas cellar seemed to used to keep her wines and beer that she was always making, it was stored in earthenware stone flagons

My Grandma brought up eleven children in this environment. Everyone should have to endure these conditions for a couple of weeks. There wound not be so much talk about the good old days. They were only good days for some.

We had to bathe in a tin bath in front of the fire. Modesty was provided by the clothes horse with a blanket round it. It was a case of first in best washed. Recycling was invented in the thirties not in the two thousands. Our toilets were the get in and tread it down style, which were across the road about fifty yards away. The toilets were in three sections a two seater at one side, a thee seater in the middle, and another two seater at the other side. Just plain deal wooden planks with oval holes, no lids.

At the back was the ash madden were we put the ashes from the fire. We did not have any dust bins in those days everything that could be burned was put on the coal fires.

Our neighbour Mrs Hakesworth was in service when she was single She used to talk about their flush toilets how she did not like them, because they stank awful especially when the master had been, she much preferred the outside toilets. The ladies kept the toilets spotlessly clean even the steps were scrubbed and (donkey stoned) ask your grandma about that.

How did we manage, well to put it in a nutshell we did not know any different, It's often said every one was honest in those days. Don't you believe it; we did not lock our doors because we had not much that was worth pinching.

However I do remember granddad getting a wireless set. I would have been about five years old at the time, the fist station to transmit was from Drioitwich, it did not have a name it had a call sign which was ' Two LO calling', the Arial was fastened to a tree about twenty five yards away, and it had to have good earth. All these radios as we now call them now were worked with valves of different values that was the case right up until about 1945, when transistors came in We had to have two volt (WET) rechargeable batteries for the filaments and a dry 120volt battery for the anodes, and think we had to have a 9 volt dry battery for the grid bias. This was about 1926-7.

The next thing that I can recall is my first day at school; I would be four years old. It was a church school and my teacher was Miss Brook, who was said to have been a teacher at Barnsley Girls High School. I remember putting my hand up to go to the toilet, and she told me I would have to wait and go at playtime. To put it bluntly I couldn't wait and I promptly shit myself. I had to walk home across the fields by myself, carrying my trousers, this culminated in my last memory of my mother, when she was remonstrating with Miss Brook about the incident. Miss Jane Brook was a grizzly old spinster who lived alone, apart from about 6 or 7 cats who never went out of her cottage. I only went once into her cottage, it smelled putrid. Her singing voice resembled a corn crake with a sore throat, but funnily enough she was in the Chapel choir.

I suppose that shortly after this would have been when my mother died in childbirth at Barnsley Infirmary. I remember my father coming home and telling my Granddad that she had gone, but I did not understand. On the day of the funeral I could not understand why all the relatives were gathering at Grandmas house, I wondered what had happened. To get us out of the way a neighbour, Arnold Beaumont, took us to Woolley Edge for a picnic in his motor-bike and side- car. Arnold and his brother Vernon were plasterers by trade, and they used what was called a box for carrying their tools and materials in. They had to take off the side-car and attach the box to the motor-bike.

After that we lived mostly at grandmas, father did not remarry again until he was about sixty. He worked at the pit on three shifts so he could not look after us but he was a very good dad, I slept with Uncle Hector in the same room as grandma and granddad. Doreen slept with auntie Cecily in the same room as aunties Mary and Nancy, I remember if we wanted to do a no two during the night , we had to get dressed and go across the road with a candle in a jam jar for or a light. We were very well looked after especially by Auntie Cecily. Grandma was a prolific wine maker and Beer brewer. There were no DIY kits then, she made several different varieties of wine, dandelion flower, elderberry flower and berry. Rhubarb, potato and also wheat (no she did not have a still, but I suspect one of the neighbours had one.) She brewed in the old fashioned way; the ingredients were put in an earthenware container (bread bin) and scalded with boiling water. Then a thick slice of toast was floated on top. Then Brewers yeast was put on that. At what stage the sugar was put in I do not know, when it had stopped fermenting it was decanted into stone jars. In her kitchen she had a bin with a semi circled lid in which she could keep about six stones of flour plain flour, self raising did not appear until after WW2. Inside the flour she would have big lumps of suet. No shredded suet then. If it was buried well in the flour it would keep a long time. In those days flour was sold in multiples of one stone and freshly weighed out in the shops The same with other provisions like butter ,sugar, margarine lard cheese and many other things, they were all weighed out in the shops. She used to buy salt in very big blocks.

Before we could use this it had to be scraped onto a tray and put into the oven to be dried out then put into salt cellars for table and cooking purposes. It also would useful for curing bacon and hams.

Granddad was a very good gardener, we lived on Allendale estate and every year there was a competition for the best garden. The winner had his name inscribed on a silver cup .It was not absent from our mantle shelf for very long. In later years his son Hector won it and, his son Bernard got his name on it. The estate provided paint to decorate the cottages. We could have any colour we wanted as long as it was green. We had to walk to Breton Estate Workshops to get it, a distance of five miles there was no bus service. Also at Breton Hall the seat of the Allendale's, there was an annual flower and vegetable show. Granddad had a gallower and flat cart to take his produce to the show which was about five miles away. He always won a lot of prizes.

There was an annual agricultural and animal show, and sheep dog trials, at Cawthorne a much bigger event, that was of all comers, granddad got a smattering of prizes and rosettes there.

I recall someone coming from Cawthorne to granddads garden and bringing some sticks of Rhubarb, granddad asked him how much did he want for them? The man said oh gives my kids a penny apiece. - He had nine kids; the rhubarb was worth about two pence.

We always had enough food manly because of the garden and grandma, and auntie Cicely cooking abilities, Auntie Cecily did not go out to work (more later),they were both very thrifty they made all their own bread and cakes. One of grandma's specialities was fish cakes she used to buy fish bits from a fishmonger who came from Cawthorne; he had a pony and a small flat cart. Another of her lovely's was her bran tea cakes they were really good.

We always had home cured bacon and ham because granddad kept pigs in the garden, I do not know how many were killed each year. Uncle Hector was a butcher and slaughrterman, and he used to kill them in the garden. They killed at night when Doreen and I had gone to bed... I remember getting early one morning and bounding down the stairs steps two at a time, when I got down I got the fright of my life because a pig's carcase was hung in the kitchen, with its head in a basin to catch the blood. I bounded back up four at a time. Uncle Hector used to cure the bacon and ham in the cellar on a stone shaped out into a shallow trough. Salt was used for both, but I believe salt peter was also used for the ham. Pigs trotters were cooked which I did not even attempt to eat, the head was boiled and used to make brawn. What happened to the offal, I do not know but it would not be wasted. We probably ate pork for two or three days. Of coarse there was no refrigeration at that time, so a lot of the bits and bats were shared by friends and neighbours we who did the same when they killed one, grandma made black pudding with the blood, I did not like it then but have made up for it since. Granddad always kept chickens (They were called hens then) in the garden, so we always had a good supply of fresh eggs in spring, summer and early autumn, they did not lay in winter though. To keep eggs from going bad they used to put them in isinglass in buckets, getting them out again was like putting your hand in snot. If you wanted to be sure that they were not bad they had to be candled, that was holing a light behind them to see whether they were addled, (BAD) I remember one year when grandma was making her batch of Christmas cakes, she had the bulk of the ingredients in the bowl, and was adding the eggs one at a time, when disaster struck, The last egg was bad, and she had betoken it straight into the mixing bowl. She must have been mortified at having to throw the whole mix away and start afresh. It would have been very disheartening apart from the financial loss.

My dad was an infantryman in the WW1,he was taken prisoner at Mons, and was incarcerated for the rest of the war he was very badly treated , flogged by the cat-o-nine- tails, which left his back a mass of wheals After Armistice day he came home weighing about six stones, nominally he would weigh about eleven stones. He was sent some where on Salisbury Plain in Wiltshire to recuperate. He then got work at North Gawber Colliery stoking the boilers I believe the boilers were to make electricity to work and to ventilate the mines, later he got an easier job down the mine as a pump attendant.

One Saturday in three, when Dad was on day shift, he would go to Oakwell Football Ground to watch Barnsley Football Club, then Doreen and I would meet up with him and he would take us for afternoon tea at

Butterfields Restaurant on Market hill. That was a real treat. Whenever we had a good meal at home Dad used to say, "that would have cost half a crown at Butterfields" (that is twelve and a half pence.) on occasion I have quoted it to my family. He also took us tithe 'first house pictures' that is what is now called the early screening at the cinema. They were silent films with sub titles and a piano for accompaniment, on the way there we called at the greengrocers for some monkey nuts 'peanuts' and some dates that were cut from a big slab.

We some times went to the local flea pit 'cinema' at Maplewell the admittance was a half penny and a jam jar! We also went to another flea pit in Barnsley were we used to see a succession of cliff hangers, one film would last about three months, each week ending on a ' cliff hanger you just *had* to go next week to see what happened.

When I was about fourteen, there were at least seven cinemas in Barnsley all very well attended in fact on a Saturday we generally had to queue a quite a while to get in. Talking Pictures came in about nineteen twenty eight. Auntie Nancy took us to the first one at the Alhambra Cinema, in Barnsley, the theme song of it was "if I had a talking picture of you-oo' Technicolor came in the late thirties.

I was told by dad that mother had a small cake and sweet shop in Darton, next to the chemists shop dad said that they had done their courting there before he enlisted. I understood that she had to close it due to the severe food rationing. My mother was born with a very severe impediment , she was born with a cleft palate and a hair lip, my sister had the same impediment which, sorry to say, her first- born David had the same, he never married, fortunately the disfigurement in our family stopped its ravages there. Granddad had a saying that he would quote; "The sins of the fathers shall be visited upon the children from generation to generation" you see grandma was the illegitimate child of a man called Bill Alcock, who was a pillar of society, He was also the granddad of my best friend Donald Alcock, granddad did not approve of our friendship. Actually a great deal of bitterness existed between the two families, Granddad seemed to lay the blame for the hair lip condition squarely on Bill Alcock. makes you think! David suffered really badly he had a double hair -lip he had to have about ten operations on it, even then he was badly hampered with his speech.

I do not remember granddad working at all. He suffered badly with all the ' isms' , 'attics ' and 'irises' I recall him going to Buxton Spa in search of some kind of therapy, it did not seem to do much good. His last job had been a coal miner at Jiggers Darton Maine a pit that was sunk on a lot of faults and was only open for a short time. An estate was built for the workers there, it was called Darton West, locally known as 'China Town" and was supposedly "Jerry Built" but as far as I know everyone is still standing However it was decimated by the pit closure.

A new Council School was built at Kexborough and the old one was closed down, in later years it became one of the first youth clubs, granddad was involved with this. I started as one of the first pupils. Our teachers were Stanley Whitely, Mr Sutton Miss Avyard and Miss Oxley apart from the latter they were alright, Miss Oxley was a bit of a tarter, and our Head master was Frank Warren. He was strict but fair. He was a very good cartoonist, and he would tell us very humorous stories about when he had been a soldier. Mr Whitely was a nap hand with a piece of chalk, he could hit a fly at twenty yards. He used his skill to good effect when, as often we were, messing about. Corporal Punishment was the 'norm' at that time I was as mischievous as any other lads and received my fair share of the cane. I only once cried about it when I had been punished for someone else.

Once I was sent down to Allots shop in Darton for a bundle of new canes ad on my return the teacher said that he had better try one out to see if it worked he therefore administerd one on my hand, I assured him that it worked alright, I had probably done something wrong to deserve it, I was no angel.

Grandma's firstborn was Uncle Charles he was a coal miner he married Sally Everest and they had three children, Norma, Mable and Raymond I can not remember much about the first two, I know that Norman went into farming, Mable went into service. Raymond went into farming and later worked in the mines, He was what I call a born miner, and I think he was capable of doing any job at a mine, even higher management. One of the managers used to consult him about different problems. He was very technically minded he would have a try at repairing anything, clocks watches radios televisions motor bikes cars, very often with success. At School Raymond was quite a ' lad', one day he managed to get some carbide crystals, he put a few in each ink well on our desks The carbide and the gas formed a gas and discharged an inky mess all over the class room I cannot recall the punishment that he received but I am certain he would wish his posterior would cool down.

Uncle George was killed by a sniper in WW1 and grandma got a pension of ten shillings a week for him. They had to have the Dreaded Means Test to qualify for it.

Uncle Clarence was next he was a gardener by trade, and was employed by Mr Badly who was the manager of Woolley Colliery. He married his first cousin Harriet, they wisely, had no children and they lived with her Mam and Dad. Auntie Minnie and Uncle Arthur. At the bottom of Old Mill Lane, Barnsley. Uncle Arthur was quite a character; I recall when I went there he used to say. '' Eye up Minnie fetch me a quart from t'off'' that meant fetch me two pints from the beer off shop, they sold draught beer to take home, that was repeated at least three times a night. I remember years later when I worked at Woolley Colliery with a man called Harry Bedford, who told me that shop was a godsend to the local people mostly miners, especially during the 1926 General strike, when they let people have ' tick' that's credit. Things were very bad then and right through to about 1936-7, when things picked up because we were preparing for WW2 "bloody barmy isn't it" amazing isn't it, money could be found for that, when for ten lousy years people had been on the bread line. I recall in1926 there was a soup kitchen at the back of the White Bear Pub at Kexborough, me and my sister took our dishes to get some. Much to our dismay we were refused, that was because our dad was working at the time He was not a scab, he had to work to keep the mine ventilated. However when grandma heard about our visit to the soup kitchen we were severely told off - 'Ellis's do not ask for charity!'

Aumtie Harriet died very young... Uncle Clarence married again to Muriel Wharam and they lived with her mother in Rockingham St Barnsley (he must have been a glutton for punishment). A lot of people did not like him; he was a bit of a cantankerous sort of a chap. I always got on well with him, whenever we met up during the war he always used to slip me a bob or two.

Uncle Hector was a butcher and slaughterman by trade. He was the manager of the Mapplewell Branch of the BBCS, on a Saturday it was my job to take his dinner to him, and collect the weekend joints of meat for grandma and dad, Dad used to have two shillings worth and grandma had three shillings worth, I used to wonder why grandmas was three times bigger than Dads. While I was there he used to get a delivery of ice for his refrigerator, it came in large oblong blocks which were put in the top of the 'fridge it was my job to break it up and put something on It. I can't remember what. I think they had the ice delivered two or three times a week.

Uncle Hector was a prolific story teller. Many unrepeatable in polite circles, one concerned an old lady who came in for some bones late on Saturday afternoon, she asked him if he had any bones such as bacon ribs ham bones, etcetera to make soup with, he parcelled few up for her, and she asked how much is that, he said it was Saturday afternoon and she could have them for nothing, the old lady said oh no I want to pay for them so that I could get my' divi'.

He could not get on with a new General Manager (who was called Hannibal) you can guess what his nickname was! He left and bought an insurance book. That did not last long, because he did not like the job. He called himself a 'graveyard bookie,' he bought a Butchers shop and Bakery at Breton West. His speciality was pork pies. Which were absolutely delicious particularly when they were straight out of the oven. He used to raise and kill his own pigs, his slaughter house was next do to the bakery , the environmental health people put a stop to that in the fifties. I recall watching him kill one (after the war) and I very near fainted at the sight of it. When I was a child I used to watch them being killed at Kexborough (where they also killed cattle) and it did not bother me at all then, when a pig was killed they use to give us the bladder to blow up to play football with 'Ugh' that was life then, we just got on with it.

Killing at that time was not very humane, it was the pole axe for cattle and the pigs and sheep had their throats cut. The pole axe was a long handled axe on the opposite side to the axe was a spike. The cow was hit in the middle of the forehead with the spike, that just stunned and dropped it so that the slaughtermen could bleed them (for the black puddings)I have seen skulls on the manure heaps with four holes in their foreheads.. Meaning some poor beast had to be hit four times before they stunned it.

Uncle Hector's wife was Gladys Knight she was a seamstress and had worked with Auntie Harriet. They had two children, Bernard and Margaret. Both worked in the bakery and the shop.

Auntie Mable and her husband Uncle Donald lived in Manningham Street Bradford, which is the steepest street that I have ever seen that had houses built on it, must have been at least one in five. They had no children; uncle was badly injured in WW1 and walked with a bad limp. He had his own picture framing business and followed in his father's footsteps. Auntie Mable was in service at a manor somewhere near Bradford, before marriage.

Auntie Nancy was in service after leaving school. She was employed by a family called Draycup of Bradford they were electrical component manufacturers. She never worked any where else and she progressed to become the housekeeper, but later on she had to leave to return home to look after grandma who developed severe dementia, and in her later years grandma became bedridden. When Grandma died she married John Liik a friend of granddad. John was a nationalised Briton he was born in one of the Baltic countries and had been at sea before settling in England, he spoke very good English. He worked at Woolley Colliery, he died at about seventy. Auntie Nancy lived to be ninety two. She was very prim and proper but she was wonderful with it, everyone loved Auntie Nancy. She never had anything out of place, and would never visit anyone empty handed, there was always a gift of some kind. Quite often it was some home made delicacy.

Auntie Cicely was the one that brought us up, she was very kind to us, she taught us good manners, some thing that I have tried to adhere through all my life. I am afraid that is sadly lacking. Nowadays. At that time after a meal it was customary for children to say, "thank you for a good meal please may I leave the table" often abbreviated to " plug- mud -uh-tub" it would do everyone good to go back for a few weeks. She married George Wareham he was an out of work colliery electrician, and they went on to run a newsagents shop in South Elmsall. I suspect that Georges Auntie La (that was her proper name) bought it for them. It was a good thriving business, I used to love going because I could read all the comics as they came out. (Free of charge). They had a cigarette machine outside there shop that dispenced two woodbines and two matches for a penny. It was well patronised by miners going to work, you see they could not take matches or cigarettes down the mine. They had two boys Anthony and Christopher. Neither continued with the business, Anthony went onto a small holding and Christopher went into the radio and television trade. When Auntie Cicely married Auntie Nancy had to come home. Things are bit different theses days.

Auntie Mary had a "I am better than you complex" and thought that she should have been born into a better life style. She worked at Beanlands Mill at Clayton West. Horace Kaye was her husband he was also a manager of BBCS butchers shop at Wath on Deurne, South Yorkshire he was a quite a self opinioned chap. He too fell out with Hannibal just before Uncle Hector, he became an agent for The Corporative Assurance Company and by all accounts became a very good agent, he got tuberculosis and had to go into a sanitaria for a while. Auntie Mary kept his insurance book open until he recovered. He had been a very heavy smoker of robin cigarettes. He gave up because of the tuberculosis.

One of my jobs in a morning was to go down to the Co-op for whatever provisions we needed that day. I usually dallied and dollied until I was late for school. The manager was Frank Morris, he was a grand chap. He was an Alderman and a Magistrate. His first assistant was Jack Brown who died fairly young of tuberculosis, very prevalent at that time. In those days the Co-operatives Societies paid dividends (Divi) out on all purchases, it was usually Two Shillings and sixpence to the pound. With each purchase we got a check, a copy was kept at head offies, these were totalled up half yearly and the dive paid out twice a year. . This was quite a boon for the holidays and at Christmas time. Every one had here own number grandmas was 2820 Dads was 44839.It must have been quite a task at head office there were no computers then...

From about eight years go age we would go on holidays to Blackpool with Grandma and Granddad, our 'digs' were 53 Palatine Road, Mr and Mrs Smith were the landlord and landlady. Granddad used to take a lot of his own garden produce, you see in those days the visitors provided their own food, and the landlady cooked for them . Imagine cooking different meals for up to ten families. It must have been a nightmare, on one occasion we were eating garden peas, and they were bit ropey. The family at the next table remarked how nice their peas were. I think you will have cottoned on what had happened. Just one lady in in the entire boarding house was a smoker, she was shunned by every one 'ladies did not smoke in public ', in those days.

Later on when I was fifteen we went to the same 'digs' with dad. I slept with dad and my sister slept with her friend Tilly Marsden. At that time I had started smoking, which dad did not know about. One evening at bedtime I asked my sister to look after my cigarette case. Next morning at breakfast, in front of my dad she handed it back to me. Dad did not appear to blink an eyelid, and for the rest of the week we were swapping cigarettes. On returning home I thought that I could carry on, oh no dad would have none of this, '' we are at home now me lad, that is different" I was not allowed to smoke in front of him for a long time.

At Kexborough our social life revolved around the Methodist Chapel an old damp building at the top of Bench Lane. We *had* to attend Sunday school, morning and afternoon, afternoon service, evening service, and prayer meeting if there was one. Monday evening was Band of Hope, Tuesday was Christian Endeavour, Wednesday was Wolf cubs or Brownies or Scouts Club Fridays we occasionally had a Faith Tea. That was when all the ladies took some kind of food; there was always a good spread of wholesome food. It was called Faith Tea; because everyone had faith that something would be provided. At Sunday school we had star cards; a star was put on for each attendance. Each summer there was a prize giving service, those who had most stars got the best prise, which were mostly religious books.

Very occasionally we were allowed to miss the Sunday Afternoon Service, on one such Sunday we went for a walk down by the River Deurne. Actually it was only a steam at that point. We tried to dam it but a lad called Clarkson fell in wearing his only 'best' suit. At this point we compounded the issue by lighting a fire to dry his cloths. They 'somehow' got burned "Oh Calamity" I can not remember what happened to us , I guess we were not very popular with his parents, but I think he would have a sore bum for quite a while.

Occasionally we had Lantern Slides (the forerunner of the projector) I only recall the subject of one, it was about the conditions of African natives, conditions do not seem to have altered more than eighty years later. Makes you think. Where have all those Billions of Aid gone. (Swiss Banks spring to mind)

On my Dads side was my Grandfather George, who I was named after He must have gone blind about the time I was born, because I have no recollection of him being able to see. He had cataracts on both eyes and he went for operations to have them removed, but he had a bad cough and they would not operate. Grandma's name was Mary. She must have died before I was born. When granddad went blind he went to live with his daughter, Auntie Ethel who was married to Earnest Wood, who will be mentioned later in this story. They had one child Geoffrey, who same as his dad was a very good pianist. Uncle Earnest died when he was only about fifty

Uncle Lawrence and his wife Peggy had three daughters Phyllis, Muriel, and Margaret, I do not remember much about them, he was badly injured at Woolley Colliery and was off work for years, however he by sheer determination got himself reasonably fit again and started working on he railway. He was a Relief Porter, another Uncle named Albert was a signalman at Goldthorpe, I only ever saw him once.

On of the local characters in our village was Old Seth Johnson, he was quite an enigma. He lived a very reclusive life in several derelict houses. He did casual work at several farms. Mostly at Bench Bottom Farm. Boys used to tease him a lot, like pelting him with snow balls. One of the houses that he lived in was easy to get onto his roof, and one particularly nasty lad blocked up his chimney. And smoked the poor old sole out.

Another whose name (I think) whose was name was Dixon was the village rouge; he was in and out of prison like a yoyo. He must have loved prison life, because he never committed any serious crime .For example he broke into shops but he never stole anything of real value.

He was apprehended very quickly and back in jug he went. In those days there were quite a few tramps, vagrants as they are now called, some had fallen on bad times, others it was a way of life. Grandma was a soft touch for them; she would often give them some food. It was usually a sandwich or a piece of cake. Granddad did not approve of it, he used to say somewhere on this house there is a mark that denotes to other tramps, that this is a good place for a bite.

At that time visiting preachers at the local chapel were 'invited' to Sunday tea by the ladies; tomatoes were not as commonplace as they are now. Granddad had just stated to grow them in his greenhouse, one Sunday some were put on the table and the parson partook of several of them, Granddad asked him "did he like them". The parson replied that he probably would when he had acquired the taste. (Granddad controlled himself).

Granddad Ellis also had cataracts he had them removed when he was about seventy five years old. He had a very wry since f humour. He had a 'pokerwork plaque'. Hung over his bed which read "All the world's a bit queer except me and thee, and I look at thee sometimes"

Sports day at school was something that we used to enjoy, There was the wheelbarrow race, egg and spoon race several distance races, relay race, three leg race, sack race, sack tournament and many others. The school was divided into four houses' Red Blue Green and Yellow, the competition was very fierce. In nineteen thirty five to celebrate the Silver Jubilee of King Edward and Queen Mary we had an inner-school Sports Competition held on the playing fields at Dalton. I managed to win the sack tournament and got a leather wallet for a prize. I have no idea how I managed it because I knocked out lads who were much bigger than me. Lady luck was on my side. The following year I entered at my own school and was demolished in the first round. We also had a Sunday school sports day which was held in the Scout Field at Kexborough my sister won a lot of prizes.

Anther happy occasion was the Annual Whit Walk, as it was called. It took place on Whit Monday and was celebrated in Cities Towns and Villages throughout Yorkshire and Lancashire. In our district it involved Kexborough, Darton, and Maplewell, all denominations participated.

We nearly all had 'new' clothes for the occasion, it was to celebrate Trinity. We used to walk around all three villages, some one from each church or chapel would carry a banner and we would sing hymns. We probably sang Onward Christian Soldiers.'

Toddy my carer and I were talking about school holidays and half terms the October Half term was called 'Tate' picking week. We were expected to go potato picking for local farmers, the lowest pay was one shilling and nine pence a day. (That's eleven an a half pence now and the *best pay* was Two and three pence a day. We had to take our own buckets, and at some of the farms we were allowed to take home two roasters (pronounced rosters) a day, at others, only the dirt in our finger nails. The large potatoes were called roasters. One of the perks was riding the horses to and from the fields.

We also helped the farmers at hay and harvest time that was for free we did a lot of larking about (as lads do.) The enjoyable part was the allowance, as the grub was called. There were ham and beef sandwiches and cakes, lemonade and home made beer, and Little Albert, -all very nice, Little Albert was a concoction of yeast sugar ginger and water, very refreshing, it could be kept going for a long time by 'feeding' it every three days, or it went 'off'.

Before long by my steam radio it will be Mischief Night (November 4th this mooning my carer reminded that it will be Bonfire night before long When was at my silly age (some say I still am) we called November 4th mischief night, this is when we got up to all kinds of misbehaviour it did not get 'malicious' very often. We would swop people's gates around, put small fireworks up drain pipes 'they made awful noises, please children do not do it now, and it could have disastrous consequences with plastic drainpipes). We would take down their cloths lines so that we could tie their front door to their back door. We did not realise that hazard that this caused. We also made window rattlers out of cotton reels, to do this we cut notches out of the edge of empty sewing cotton reels put a long length of string around the reel put a stick through the reel, put the reel up to the window, and pull the string it made a terrifying noise to the occupants. If we got caught we expected to get a clout round the ear, and never dream of complaining. The weeks before Bonfire night we collected wood and rubbish fore the occasion. It had to be hidden because different gangs would go round pinching it. This some times resulted in fisticuffs, black eyes and burst noses and thick ears were exchanged. However don't forget you are never given black eyes, you usually have to fight for them...

Farming nowadays is no bed of roses any means, but in my youth it was dammed hard long laborious man hours, there was very little machinery, it was all britches arse steam. All farms had a lot of horses, usually heavy Shires. Tractors were very thin on the ground, there were non in our district. The first tractor I saw was one with iron wheels, they were not allowed on the road. Ploughing the fields needed two horses to plough a single furrow. When reaping the corn it required three horses to pull the binder (only a five foot cut) it was called a binder, it cut the corn a tied it into sheaths, which in turn had to be put into stookes about ten sheaths to a stook, when was dry it was taken by horse and dray to the stockyard to await the thrashing machine. This was hired as required. The thrashing machine was belt driven by a steam traction engin,e the engine had to be strategically placed so that the sparks did not set fire to the other stacks. The resulting corn was put into **two hundredweight sacks, that's a hundred kilos** and carried up about twelve steps to the grain store it must have been back breaking work (the saying strong in the back, weak in the head springs to mind) When the corn stack was near to the ground the farm dogs were in their element, waiting for the rats to flee from there very cosy and fruitful homes, very few survived.

Haymaking was very similar; the edges of the fields were opened up by scythes to enable the mowing machine to come in. The grass was cut when it was still a bit green. It was left till next day to wilt when it was turned over a time or two by a machine to get the moisture out of it. Then it was raked up ad put into haycocks, to be collected by horse and dray to be stacked and thatched near to the farm, very occasionally haystacks caught fire due to spontaneous combustion, usually because some green grass had bee missed.

'Tatie' picking was back breaking work the potatoes were spun out of the ground by a horse drawn spinner which spread them over a five foot width. They were put into sacks for immediate use, if not they were put into a 'pie'. First of all a layer of soil was taken out and put on one side, then a thick layer of straw was put down. Then the potatoes were formed into a long tapered mound another layer of straw was put on top and then thatched to allow the rain to run off, this was then covered by the earth that had bee removed, this insulated it from the frost, only sound potatoes were put in bad ones could have caused a lot of rotting.

In those days all cows were milked by hand. Which in winter was in a nice warm cowshed. In summer when they were grazing in green pastures their bowels were very loose. Unfortunately, if you were at the back of a cow when it coughed, you would be sprayed by a stream of very fluid cow shit. I can assure you it was not a pleasant experience.

At school my favourite subjects were history and geography, I can not say they did me any good in later life. The history was mostly ancient stuff. I recall when we had a supply teacher who tried to teach us some modern history, starting with the Boer War, WW1, and also the Abyssinian War that was going on at that time, it was different, *he* seemed to enjoy it.

During this period of my life there were a great amount of pit disasters mostly gas explosions. The one I remember most vividly was at Woolley Colliery. It happened in the Thorncliffe seam. The coal face caught fire and the face had to be sealed off, I do not know whether there were any casualties at that point. The face was sealed off to starve the fire of oxygen. After quite long period it was decided that the fire would have gone out, and so a decision was made to reopen the face. This had to be done with stop watch precision when rev-ventilating it again. However the fire had not been quelled, an enormous explosion took place killing the Pit Manager Mr Badley and two under managers plus several more workers. You see a massive build up of gas had accumulated, and when the face was reventillated the oxygen and the methane combined into an explosive mixture between seven and eleven per-cent, and with the fire not being extinguished it went up with a massive blast. I do not think the face was ever reopened. There must have been another bad explosion at Woolley Colliery. Very near to that one, because a large number of Kexborough Cricket team were killed in it, and many others in the district. There was a gas explosion at North Gabber Colliery and at numerous other pits I do not know a lot about them. This I do know in those days, in my, and others opinions was that profit,....that came before lives!

Granddad Ellis used to tell the story about a certain woman MP called Lady Aster, she was on Wakefield Station when the Deurne Valley express train came into the station, that was the train the Deurne Valley colliers used from the Deurne valley pits, She was apparently appalled at the ragamuffin appearance of the miners, you see there were no pit head baths at that time, and a lot of them would not have baths at home either. She said "**My word, do they let them out**" no wonder there was a general strike in 1926 with people of that kind ruling the country, and still the poor sods had to go back to work for less money, as had happened marry limes before.

At Darton West, the out of work colliers had a jazz band, they made own instruments 'Tommy talkers' they were called. They went all over to take donations for the strike funds.

In the late twenties (I think) granddad woke me up one night to watch the spectacular Aurora Borealis (northern lights) I really thought that the world was coming to an end they were quite wonderful. It was the only time I and many others would see them. Around the same time there was a total eclipse of the sun, it happened in the afternoon, I was at my Cousin Raymond's house and I remember Norman taking me home. It was fully dark, I don't think that it had been publicised much, because the lamp lighter was lighting the gas lamps.

Then what I think was when the Kings Cup Air Race took place. We were bang in the middle of the course, we could not have a better view, we lived at the edge of the village as they were coming towards us. And they seemed very low, about two hundred and fifty feet; there were a lot of them. We could see the pilots quite clearly. A grandstand view.

Also at that period I saw an Autogiro that was on display at Breton Hall Park Flower Show. That was the predecessor of the Helicopter and the only other I have ever see, has been on the goggle box.

Going back to my time at the Church School. Alan Cobham's Flying Circus was displaying at Staincross, about five or six miles away. There was one coming towards us, and there was time to get us all into the playground to see it flying overhead. It was a long time before we were to see another.

I can not remember a winter in my early childhood when we did not get a lot of snow and icy conditions, I remember on day shovelling my way to school, which was about a quarter of a mile away. I got almost there when someone told me it was closed. At that time Electric Blankets were not even thought about, to warm our beds, hot cast iron oven plates were wrapped up in an old towel and were propped up in bed .They worked a treat. Also stoneware hot bottles were used to good effect. But sore shins and bruises were a hazard with those.

There were not many people who boasted wall to wall carpeting at that time, almost everyone had rag rugs, and underneath them we had linoleum or the cheaper version oilcloth. The rugs were made fro m old clothes that were pegged into 'Harding' Hessian on a wooden frame. I will attempt to explain how it was done, we made a frame and Hessian was nailed to one end and at the other end was a roller to enable to keep it tight. The cloth was cut into pieces one inch wide and about four inches long We had a pointed piece of mettle or hard wood and a hole was made in the Hessian and one end of the rag was pushed through, another hole was made at the side of that and from underneath the end of the rag was pulled through to the front, etcetera ad lib, it kept idle fingers from getting into any other mischief. So my grandma said, if you wanted to make a patterned rug you could buy bags of different coloured rags, ready cut up, on Barnsley Market.

Barnsley was a proper market town there were five regular markets on Tuesdays and Saturdays. There was a fish market, situated in a triangle at the side of Woolworth's stores. The Vegetable and fruit market was on Mayday Green. The meat market was on Market Hill. There was a clothes and haberdashery market by the Bus Station. There was also a Market by the power station when the travelling fair was not in residence. On Saturday evenings you could get some real bargains, the reason being that they had no refrigeration at that time and the butchers and the Fish Mongers in particular had to clear there stalls.

Mentioning rag rugs reminds me of an occurrence when I was in the RAF. I was on leave staying at my mother-in-laws home, and at the time I was making model planes, carving them with a penknife. And my young brother-in-law was helping? me in the very cold kitchen. When my mother -in-law said ''if you will promise to clear up when you have done you can come a do it on the rug in the front room" When we had finished, later in the evening, we took the rug outside to shake it. Unfortunately with our vigorous shaking, we came back in with two rugs instead of one. If there had been a mouse hole I would have been in it in two seconds. More than likely the Hessian was second hand, more than likely an old farmers sack, and obviously it could not withstand the vigorous shaking that we gave it, you see new Hessian was being used to make sandbags during the war "Oh Calamity" I do not think I was very popular with Ma-in law, I think I got away with it because the favourite son was involved.

Every year we had to have the chimney swept, usually the sweep would arrive at six clicklock in the morning. Even at that time he was "as black as the proverbial sweep' he probably had a bath once a month whether he needed it or not! Granddad kept the soot to mix with lime to use as a fertiliser for the garden. It had to be 'weathered' for a year before it could be used.

The slops from the 'gazunders' (chamber pots) were taken into his garden by granddad for watering his fruit trees. I have never tasted better apples in my life, also they kept well, there were not many weeks in the year when did not have apples.

One of my jobs was to tear up newspapers into squares and then thread them onto a string to hang up on a nail in the privy. It made interesting reading, it was very boring when toilet rolls came in, all they read was Izal Izal Izal, Wash your hands now. Granma taught me to crumple up the paper to make it softer to your bottom. No we did not use shiny magazines. As a family we always ate together at the table, sadly often that is not the case now .When we had guests the smaller children had to eat in the kitchen,we did not like this, probably because we were scared of missing some juicy gossip. However were always very well fed.

The kitchen did not have a white enamelled sink like most people had at the time. Ours was made out of very smooth stone; quite shallowly chilled-out it was badly worn at the front where knives had been sharpened. A white enamelled bowl was used to wash up in, this doubled up for many purposes, rice puddings, baking bread and cakes, even for mustard footbaths. In dire water shortages no water was wasted, water from the washing up and baths would be used to water the garden. Granddad used to collect rainwater from his three greenhouses, pigsty and shed, in large wooden barrels which had previously contained onions from Spain. They stank awful until the whiff faded with age. During dry periods he used to carry water in buckets to the garden, milkmaid fashion to balance them and to stop them banging into his legs. It was a fair distance to the garden about one hundred and fifty yards.

The house that we lived in was part of the Allendale Estate whose owners also owned Bretton Hall Park, the Hall was later turned into an art college. The park contains some very 'interesting' abstract sculptures by various artists, including the Yorkshire man Henry Moore. At one time there was fairly big lake in he park, but it was drained due to underground mine workings, it was never filled up again to my knowledge.

Village roads were lit by gas lamps; these were mantle lamps that gave off about twenty candle power. Originally they had to be lit and extinguished each day by a lamplighter who had to carry a ladder around to enable him to do his job, later a bit of automation came in, and a pilot light was continually burning. And a wind up clock was installed in each one. The lamplighter was not made fully redundant he still had to put new mantles on, clean the glass and adjust the timing. In those days the Milky Way was clearly visible and we also saw quite a few shooting stars. Today's street lighting has put paid to that.

In the late twenties there was a severe Diphtheria out break in the village, I think that quite a few people died, the council had to fumigate many buildings, this blackened the brickwork consequently this meant at school we were given IZAL tablets which we had to suck, they tasted horrible, but I do not remember any one spitting them out, we must have known that they were a necessary evil. The situation was extremely serious, and we knew that it was important to suck these awful things. At tat time under privileged children received footwear and clothing it must have been a hell of a stigma, but they gratefully excepted it (Needs must, when the devil drives)

Also at that time there were a lot of other very infectious diseases about, scarlet fever, chicken pox, two types of measles, whooping cough, TB, polio, mumps, thanks to our wonderful NHS nearly all these have disappeared. One of the newspaper magnets supplied iron lungs for polio victims. A lot of children and adults had to go to isolation hospitals.

Milk, in those days was delivered by hand from oval shaped cans and ladled out in pint and half pint measures into your own containers. The farmers in our village did it themselves (well usually by their wives and daughters).they carried the cans fastened to a yoke one on each side to keep balance. I cannot remember when milk bottles came to be used in our village, but it was at least in the late thirties. I used to fetch our milk from the local farm in an enamel vessel with a lid and a swinging wire handle. Yes you have guessed what is coming haven't you? I used to swing the can over my head (clever but not when the handle comes off) I probably got a hand applied sharply to my arse1. One day when I was going for the milk one of the lads next door gave me a truepenny bit to get him five woodbines from the shop (five woodbines were two pence then) unfortunately I lost the coin, we soured the footpath for quite a while. To no avail...

In the use days Chicken was something that was only eaten for Christmas Dinner, occasionally we would have a boiling fowl, but only when it had ceased laying, Granddad used to say we might as well eat as feed it.

In the thirties depression, we stated to get free milk at school, it came in one third of a pint bottles, we drank it through a straw or straight from he bottle. We had to take turns to be milk monitor, Jack green was the first, when he was older he worked for BBCS who supplied the school milk. That nice Mrs Thatcher up a stop to that in the late nineteen seventies

Harry Booth was the ink monitor. He would clean and fill the ink wells every Friday afternoon (no rubber gloves then0, why his mother put up with it I don't know. He wore an apron for the job but he used to finish up like he was going for an audition for the Black and White Minstrel show.

Not many people had telephones in their homes; I do not remember when telephone booths came in, probably mid thirties. Those who did have telephones had to go through an operator at a telephone exchange, it was said that the operators were busy bodies who listened in on peoples conversations. It must have been difficult when you needed a doctor. I didn't have a telephone until I bought my first business in 1963

Sometimes I am envious of how lucky children of today are, and then I think of what they are missing, and realise that we were a lot better in some respects, a lot of them are missing their precious childhood. We could go out in the streets and countryside at any time of day, being careful that we did no damage to the farmers property. Our parents were not unduly worried about our safety. In my opinion crime is no worse now than it was then, the media, between them have scared people, and they have blown it out of all proportion. The games we used to enjoy were endless. Marrbles, conkers (dangerous ha ha), ring toe (which is now called hoopla) Yo Yo, Diablo, skipping , hopscotch, fives , tin can squat, cats cradle, hide 'n' seek, cigarette cards, whip and top, and of coarse doctors and nurses, plus numerous others. We were occasionally? naughty, we would go to the fish for a pennyworth of chips , then go to the other chip shop, to top up with salt and vinegar. - then run like hell for leather home, as a rare real treat we would have a fish and a pennyworth dependent on having earned a few coppers by running errands for neighbours..

After a lot of pestering of our parents, one day my friend Donald and I were allowed to camp out for the night. We wanted to do this to get a badge on our scout uniforms. We camped about half a mile away from the village, in the Pit Hills near High Holland. These hills were actually heaps of debris that had been excavated from Bell Pits. These were small coalmines worked by Monks in the middle ages. We knew that we had to be vigilant because some of the shafts were not filled in. The fences around them were a bit flimsy and one day a horse had fallen in. and was drowned. The shafts were not very deep. They were exposed by opencast mining in the 1950's. We were so exited; you would have thought we were going to the moon. However expectation was better than realisation, and the weather tuned a bit inclement. Also a nosey cow pestered us for a while. Early in the night we were disturbed by what we thought was a wild animal. It was probably a stray cat! So we upped sticks went home and were tucked up in bed well before it was time to get up. Can't imagine that we spoke about it at school with other lads, well we would not want to be called 'cowardly custards' or such like would we? However we did get our badges.

At school I seemed to be pretty good at exams, I recall I was nearly always finished well before the others. Therefore I was put forward for an entrance examination for admittance to Barnsley Grammar School. On the day of examination I was a victim of a crowd of bullies led by a blather -of -lard called Donald Horsfield who I could have knocked spots off at any time, when he did not have his cronies with him, he was a fully fledged coward, however they outnumbered and unnerved me and I failed the examination, very much to my headmasters surprise. I was put through again for what was called a George Beaumont Scheme; I have no recollection of how the scheme worked, it was probably some form of scholarship. Unfortunaty I was taken ill and missed my second chance.

At this time there as hardly any traffic on the roads and in fact about half a mile out side the village was a very rough section of the road. Actually in one place there was a spring in the middle of the road. Which was worked to our advantage? Some years, when there was a drought and no water was coming through the tap (We were at the end of the line) I think it was my granddad who made a hole at the side of the spiting , large enough to ladle it out to enable us to fill a bucket for the household use. At times it was a godsend.

We were quite naughty then, we played Cricket in the street, small holes were knocked in the road to put the stumps in, thanks to Uncle Hector and some other 'grown ups' who used to play with us, there was one bus and two cars that came through the village. We knew almost to the minute when they were due. On belonged to Victor Auckland who was an optician in Barnsley. He came from a wealthy family, and if he caught us playing she would stop and have a game with us. The other belonged to Miss Wintour, who live at High Holland she was a magistrate in Barnsley and was a stickler. She caught us on more than on occasion playing cricket and complained to my granddad, she must have considered that I was a 'wrong one' and she demanded that my granddad should thrash me. He told her that he may thrash me, but not for her, or in front of her. He did not punish me on that occasion, but on another occasion he did give me some belt for going collecting rubbish for bonfire night, instead of coming straight home from school. However after a couple of strokes Auntie Cicely intervened and I was never thrashed again.

At Kexborough the bus service was run by Mr Outran who owned just one bus that came directly to our row of houses and then tuned round, I do not know how frequent the service was. Later the Yorkshire Traction Bus Company took over, an ran an hourly service to Barnsley , service No 92, a distance of about four miles, the fare was four pence, it started at seven o'clock in the morning and finished at ten o'clock at night. They also ran a service No 38 from Barnsley to Holmfirth and another service was No 15 from Barnsley to Huddersfield, they all came through our village. The Yorkshire Traction Company took over ninety per cent of the independent bus services near Barnsley. One of the exceptions was Cawthorne's of Darton, and as far as I know they are still in existence as coach operators.

The local farmer cum joiner cum undertaker cum choirmaster, Mr Dick Smith owned an open topped charabanc, seating about thirty six persons. This had a hood for inclement weather, capable of coming right over the top. It was called Happy Days. This was used for outings. Trips to the seaside etcetera. I remember grandma going to Danby Dale Pie day in it, (more about that later in the story).

The department stores used a method of paying which would seem quite unusual if seen today. You gave your money to the assistant who was serving you. They would place it in a container which was sent to the cashier using a system of pulleys and runners. The cashier sat in an elevated position, the cashier would reverse the procedure to return your change and receipt. Nearly all transactions were made using cash. Bank accounts were very rare. The stores in Barnsley that used this system were the BBCS more commonly known as the Co-op situated at the top if Peel Street, and Butterfields at the top of Market hill. Nowadays some supermarkets use a similar vacuum method to transport the cash from the tills to the cash office. Also hospitals use this system to transport things, such as blood and samples to the laboratories.

I attended Kexborough Council School until I was about thirteen and a half, when a new school was built at Darton; I think it was called Darton Secondary School. I do not remember a lot about it, one thing I do recall I had to write an essay of my own choice. I chose the workings of the two stroke and four stroke petrol engines. I got all my information from a reference book, although I enjoyed writing the essay, and received good marks for it at the time, I did not fully understand it However when I joined the Royal Air Force we had to study this subject and I found my meagre previous knowledge stood me in good stead. Some of the knowledge must have sunk in, funny isn't it?

At Darton School we had an hour break for dinner, it was about a mile and a half from home, so we had to take sandwiches for dinner (no school dinners then) we had time to go into Darton Village. And very occasionally we would visit Wagstaff's bakery. The cream slices there were absolutely delicious they cost two pence each. On day my friend and I went in, but we only had a penny each. Mrs Wagstaff must have felt sorry for us, because we came out with one each, as we were coming out of the shop she said, don't try it again you little buggers. At one of the local pits there were some slurry beds , these were small man made ponds into which the residue from the washing screens was put to settle, eventually the water evaporated and coal briquettes were then made from residue . However, in winter they would freeze over. One of the lads from school ventured onto it, and the ice gave way. It was not very deep so he managed to scramble out, very wet, very black, and when he got home he most likely had a very sore bottom.

When we lived with grandma we had a few chores to do. On Saturday mornings I had to clean all the boots and shoes, and polish the linoleum floor, grandma used to say "do all the corners and sides, and the middle will do itself" I used to think it's a big middle. Doreen had to polish the cutlery (no stainless steel or chromium in those days) and polish all the brasses. One other task of mine during the week was tuning the mangle to iron the sheets. . Grandma did not iron the sheets , in those days there were no electric irons , she had to heat the irons on the coal fire , grandma had a chromium slipper to put on the bottom of the irons to keep the iron clean, not every one had one ,I don't know how they kept the clothes clean . Much later on ,gas and charcoal irons came in but they were big clumsy things.

My sister left school at fourteen she was unable to get a job, I think mostly because of her impediment, she had serious difficulties with her speech. No doubt grandma and Auntie Cicely would try to keep her occupied. Shortly after that we were allocated a new council house. What a difference. Electricity and gas, inside toilet and bathroom plus hot and cold running water, it was indeed absolute luxury, but compared to these days it was slightly archaic, we had a coal fired copper in the kitchen this was the boiler in which we washed our clothes. We had a wash tub, poser, rubbing board and mangle, just the same as grandma.

Doreen stayed at home to look after dad and me; I think she also helped out at a local farm.

I left school at foutee n years of age, and I was out of work for a short timet, I could have got a job down the mine but my dad was against that idea. I wanted to be a joiner, but I could not find any one to employ me. Earnest Wood who was my dad's brother-in- law was the Station Master at Haigh Railway Station informed me that there was a vacancy for a junior porter at Crigglestone West station. I applied for the job and had to go for an interview to Manchester where I had medical, vision, and intelligence tests, I needed three character references, I got one from Frank Warren my head master which was brilliant, one from Henry Walker a local solicitor and another from Gad Hepworth the local Postmaster, who was also the local home coal delivery man for the miners. He had a small lorry it would only carry a ton of coal. The miners who were allowed a ton of coal each month, at the cost of half a crown, plus haulage. If the coal was delivered to anybody other than the miner, the miner was severely reprimanded, maybe even sacked. Before the lorry it was delivered by horse and cart.

However I have digressed somewhat (its not *too* painful!) I did get the job as Junior Porter, and started on the magnificent wage of sixteen shillings a week (seventy five pence now) the terms of my employment were to be a six day working week of forty eight hours. I started at nine fifteen in the morning and finished at six fifteen at night. With an hour for lunch. I was allowed free travel to work until I was eighteen.

I received no increase in wages until I was sixteen, when I got two whole shillings a week rise. That occurred annually until I was twenty years old. I never reached the adult wage level, because I volunteered for the Royal Air Force when I was nineteen. The adult wage for a porter was thirty nine shillings and sixpence a week, with an extra one and sixpence a week if you worked in the London area. It was called cost of living allowance. I understand that this cost of living allowance for those who work in London still applies.

My Junior Porter duties included the cleaning, trimming and filling the paraffin lamps in the offices waiting rooms and platform lamps, This was not a very pleasant job, very smelly and dirty, especially on cold winter nights I did not like winters in those days, and when I get to be your MP ,I shall have them done away with. One of my other tasks was more pleasant; I had to deliver parcels in the village, when they were small. I took them on my bike, big ones I had to use a cast ironed wheeled hand cart. And the village was up the hill. However it was rewarding, the tips were very nice, but, they unfortunately started me down the path of being a smoker. Now I am suffering for it. One of my best tippers was a 'packy' not the modern term 'packy' a packy was someone who sold clothes from door to door, they were very popular in those days, they would come to your home and measure you up for a suit or an overcoat, and you could pay for them at two bob a week, with missings, if you were hard up. They were also called tally men. One if the adult porters somehow found out my source of good tips, and for a couple of weeks he was delivering the parcels himself before I got to work. When the Station Master got to know about thus he was very cross. He confronted the porter and gave him two options, he could either give me ten bob (shillings) a week for three weeks or he would sack him. He chose the former. Jobs were thin on the ground at that time.

Another duty was writing out invoices for wagons of coal and coke that were sent out from Crigglestone East. Which came from Crigglestone Colliery, which produced a type of coal that made good blast-furnace type coke. The coke was produced on site by Benzol and Bye Products.

They supplied Appleby and Framingham, Barrow in Furness and Milo Iron and Steel works. They also produced lots of bye products and of coarse Benzene which was similar to Petrol.

My times at work meant that my social life was seriously lacking by the time I got home, had a meal and got changed out of my uniform, it was about eight o'clock. Football and cricket matches were out of the question. There was little I could do about it. We got a new Station Master and he saw my point of view, and he got my hours altered to an hour earlier, which was an improvement. The Station Master had to get permission from Head office in Manchester. .

When we were about sixteen my friend Donald and I bought a tandem cycle (second hand of course) it was a monster. Normally they weighed about forty pounds; this one weighed seventy two pounds. It was made by New Hudson Bicycle Co; it was double framed and was like driving a tank. Downhill's we could break the sound barrier. We did not keep it very long.

Even then we knew that war was looming we knew that eventually we would be called up. Donald said that he preferred the Navy; I said that I would like to join the Royal Air Force. The thought of the Army and especially bayonets horrified me, as said in Dad's Army, they don't like it up 'em, and I certainly did not fancy it.

About then my sister got in the family way, and had to get married, John Harris was her husband. She had a white wedding at Darton Church, All her Aunties rallied round and it was a lovely occasion, her friend Winnie Graham and my girl friend Bessie Clegg were bridesmaids, and I was an usher. She went to live at Siltstone near Barnsley. For her it was like going back to the medieval times, no gas, no electricity, and very little water. Also she had to live with his parents who were not very nice with her. Goodness only knows he she tolerated it.

After that dad and I were on our own, we muddled along for a while, it was made more difficult because we were on different shifts and saw very little of each other. Eventually dad advertised for a live in housekeeper, and eventually after turning one or two down, he employed Nellie Brown. Who was a really nice person! And got, and kept the house, and us, in pristine condition. You see we had slipped into slovenly ways, she soon strengthened us up. She was a very competent cook, she could soon have a meal rustled up, one of her specials was mackerel pie, since then I have made it several times but I have never been able to equal her excellence, she must have used ingredient X. I think my dad threw his cap at her, but she must have thrown it back, she stayed with us for a couple of years. I think that there was a bit if gossip about them, I cannot imagine that she left because of that. She had to leave to work at munitions factory.

Doreen had five children; David was born with a double hair lip ad a cleft palate. (He had to have about ten operations to try to put it right, even then he was far from overcoming his impediment. He became an overseer on railway maintenance. Sheila was next and she worked in a bank. Next was Peter who was a mine engineer, he is now a Consultant Engineer and travels the world trouble shooting. Bernard was next he went to university to read languages, surprisingly he became a tax inspector, and he is now in the Tax Fraud Department. Irene was the last, soon after she left school she came to work for my wife and me in Blackpool where we had a private Hotel 'Homestead' .One day I tried to have a bit of humour with her, I said 'well Irene yesterday I stuck up for you '', Bob next door said, you were not to live with the pigs, I said that you were. She simply did not see the humour in that and would not speak to me for a few days. However she was a good worker and she was a big help to us that period. We were very busy. More about the Private Hotel later.

Back to my miss spent youth. Incidentally I did not get to wear long trousers until was thirteen and a half. Our chief pastimes consisted of playing cricket and football and going to the youth clubs. We did a lot of walking especially on Sunday evenings which we loved to do if the weather was fine, about six or seven of us used to walk to Cawthorne then on to Barnsley .Then back to Kexborough which was about 10 miles, we had one mouth organ between us we must have swapped quite a bit of spit... During the week we would walk to Cawthorne quite often in the evenings, we would hang around the village shop cum post office cum café and ice-cream parlour. A few likely lasses worked there and some of them lived in. We used to sit on his widow call under the girls bedroom. And chat away until quite late. One evening the girls must have got fed up with our chattering, they emptied a bucket of fluid over us, it was quite salty. I got to know afterwards that it was not (PEE) it was just salty water. From the age of fifteen and a half onwards we would go on the 'bunny run' on a Sunday evening, there were three one at Danby Dale, one at Darton and another at Barnsley. These were on stitches of roads, when the girls would walk in one direction and the boys would walk in the other direction, occasionally we would click. The one at Danby Dale was from Scisset to Danby Dale where four pubs were on the route, I can not recall any bother, (A bit different now) mostly because we did to have the money to frequent the pubs, and the one at Darton was from Borough to Darton about one and a half miles long. The one at Barnsley was on Eldon St, up Market Hill and down Burlington Arcade. A diversion was down Back Regents St, were there was a Temperance Bar where non alcoholic drinks were sold. The owner was Billy Wright. Barnsley Footfall Club's captain. The first alcoholic drink I had was in the Prospect Hotel at Danby Dale I just gone sixteen then. I slid in between two older lads and sat in a comer with half a pint of mild, I did not like it but I was a 'man' then.

It was on the Scisset 'bunny run" that I met my future wife Bessie Clegg and started courting. Our courting was done on Saturday evenings at the Skelmanthorpe (shat) cinema. Courting seats when available, and walking on Sunday evenings, (weather permitting I would cycle to Danby Dale) to save money. The bus fare was eight pence return, however I found out that if I booked to Scisset then to Danby Dale and I could save a whole penny (well it's no good being called a Tight Yorkie and not living up to their principals is it?) Think on, my spending money from my dad was only three shilling a week. (15 pence), however it was supplemented by my tips, which my father allowed me to keep. Also when I started my Relief job, he let me keep my expences. That made me comparatively wealthy.

Bessie's parents were Basil and Ado Clegg .they had three daughters and one son, Gladys and Anna were twins and they were cheese and chalk both in looks and personality. Then came Bessie two years later, and Gordon four years later. Basil was an amature all-in wrestler so were Gladys and Bessie. Basil haven trained by Dougie Clark a well known local wrestler, who had the build of a brick shit house wall. Basil used to tell about Dougies strength, he once came across an Austin seven car, which had run into a ditch. And they were going to send for help to get it out when along came Doggie and he lifted it out by himself. Wrestling then, is like today it's all a sham. You win this week and I will win next week. They all went wrestling at fairgrounds. Mr King was a fairground Wrestling Booth promoter, and he would throw out a five pound challenge for another person to take on one of his wrestlers, Bessie and Gladys used to take turns to be the challenger, also they would take turns who won. The same with Basil, the men would have their little circle of contenders with the same procedure. When they entered contests in a public building it would be a bet more genuine, it was not very often that any one got hurt. Basle trained a local farmer Hector Buckley of Dry Hill Farm Dunkirk, to wrestle, (more about Hector later in the story.) I would go and watch them wrestling o an old mattress in one of the barns. Hector was one of the farmers that I supplied with twelve bore shotgun ammunition during the war(thereby hangs a tale) I remember coming home on leave once at harvest time and going up to the farm to watch them reaping the corn. Hector shoved a gun in my hand and told me to keep an eye open for the rabbits popping out of the corn This happened towards the end of the proceedings, the reaper went round the field in ever decreasing circles until the rabbits would make a bolt for a safer home, the rabbits must have heard on the grapevine that 'Wyatt Harp' was on the prowl, so they had upped sticks and gone earlier. There was a grand total of zero. Bessie had to throw away the pastry she had made for the rabbit pie.

When I was about eighteen and a half I was given a relief porters job and I was paid the difference between a juniors wage and the wage of the person that I was relieving. I probably was paid about thirty shillings a week (that's £1.50 now) plus I got free travel for me and my bike. If I could not travel by train I got twenty minutes to the mile travelling allowance. (That was railway miles. I was decently well off.

I will always remember the day when I found out that my sister had ironed my railway uniform trousers. It was only after I got to work and got funny looks that I realised that she had ironed with the creases at the side like cowboys chaps, instead of down his centre.

The Station Master Mr Bishop, who used to think a lot of me, enquired from the authorities if they would allow me to go to commercial classes; normally only clerks were allowed to go. You see he thought that I should have been a clerk. Anyhow permission was granted. The classes were at Leeds Central Station at the top of a new building. We had to go in our own spare time, I only went for one year, after that the rooms were taken over for top management and Station Masters who went to be instructed on Air Raid Precautions, that was in 1938 everyone knew that WW2 was imminent. By the way I was very pleased to hear that I had passed the commercial class with good marks. The pass rate was sixty per cent I got seventy two per cent. It was about this time when conscription was started. All these things made a mockery of that bit paper that Neville Chamberlain flashed about. When he arrived back from speaking to Adolph Hitler, declaring ''Peace in our time' what a lot of bullshit that was. Several lads from our village were conscripted. The two names that come to mind were Cyril Aucock, the brother of my best friend. And Clarence Grayham, brother of my sisters best friend, Cyril went into the medical corps, because of his eye sight. I recall Frank coming home on his first leave; he was marching around swinging his arms up to his shoulders as if he was on parade. They both survived.

About this time Anderson Shelters arrived on the scene for the air raids that we knew would happen. These were very strong arch-shaped corrugated steel sections. DIY erections of course. A hole had to be dug in the ground, which was six foot wide eight foot long and three foot deep. The shelter was then assembled and placed in the hole, and the soil from resulting hole was earthed on top and sides. They were named after the existing Home Secretary, Sir James Anderson. They were smelly uncomfortable damp things, but they probably did save a lot of lives. Also in many towns and cities communal shelters were built, in London the Underground Tube Stations were used on a nightly basis particularly during the Blitz. After the war the Anderson shelters made good strong garages. Three or more were required to do this. There is still one in use near this village.

Shortly after the war started I volunteered for the Royal Air Force. Air Crew. And Donald Volunteered for the Royal Navy. I do not think he did much sailing; he was stationed in Iceland intercepting radio messages from U-boats etctera. probably something to do with enigma. He was sworn to secrecy on very severe consequences if he divulged anything. It would have been a treasonable offence.

I had to go to Padgate near Waddington to be assessed for the duties I was to perform, I passed the medical and the intelligence test and was selected to be a Wireless operator and air gunner, much to my disappointment, I'd wanted to be a pilot. I think my mathmatics, would have let me down, a month later I received notification that I was to report to Padgate before 12 noon on the eleventh of November. I set off from Darton Station on the 08.05 train to Wakefield, then on to Manchester Exchange and on to Padgate arriving in good time. As we were all volunteers conditions were pretty manageable for us, how could we grumble when we were volunteers. We looked a very motley lot, but if you think about it, it was the delinquent youths that considerably contributed to "winning" the war, especially the Battle of Briton.

However some bright sparks were soon misquoting one of Winston Churchill's speeches " Never - in the field - of human conflict - have so many - been buggered about - by so few - for such a long time."

The chief reason for us to be at Padgate was to be kitted out. We were not measured for any thing. We had to form a queue and when our turn came, a Sergeant said to the store man a certain size, the store man gave us the appropriate items.

First of all was a kit bag, so we could stuff every thing into it. First of all was webbing and back packs and a water bottle, one greatcoat, one ground sheet cum gas cape, one jacket (Yes only one), one pair of trousers (I did not get another pair for a long time) we must have stunk a bit high before then, three vests three shirts, three underpants, three pair of stockings one pair of gloves, two pairs of heavy boots. And shoe brushes which I still have ,and a shaving brush and razor, a knife fork and spoon and plate a gas mask and a emergency first aid kit (that we had to carry at all times), and a button stick and a hussif, see if you can work out what the last items were.

There were an army of ladies tailors on the camp to alter out clothes, which in my case were a decent fit; the trousers were a bit long. Then we got our service number 1483699 it has been imprinted on my mind ever since.

My first breakfast was repulsive; it was porridge made with water and braised pigs kidneys, I though if this is going to be the measure of RAF food then I am going to be a deserter before long. Thankfully, three days later we were transferred to Blackpool. And were billeted in boarding houses, life became more bearable.

Our first digs were in Adelaide Street which were not brilliant. Mind you we were no angels. On one occasion we set fire to the lounge carpet for which we all had to do jankers. We set the carpet on fire when we were cleaning our boots, hopefully we thought that to get a better shine on our boots , we plastered a lot of boot polish on our boots and then melted it with a candle to fill up the dimples in the leather, unfortunately some of it dripped off and set fire to the carpet, in our naïve minds we thought that if we rearranged the furniture we could get away with it (do pigs fly?), a day or two of jankers brought us back to earth.

The boots were a source of big blisters to some of the lads, mine were all right. One of the lads wore his civvies shoes for a week, and did not get caught.

However we were not there very long before we were transferred to Charnley road off Coronation Street. Mrs Charles worth was the landlady and was very kind to us, and fed us well, especially considering the food rationing (which was to get a lot worse as the conflict went on) She had two maids, one was a bit liberal with her affections, but the other was not in the front line when good looks were dished out (who am I to criticise)

We all had to be in, and the lights were put out promptly at ten thirty. There was no leeway with the lights; she had a master switch which tuned off all the bedroom lights. The whole house was clean. And the beds were comfortable. However we had to forget all about our modesty, it was two in a bed whether or not we liked it.

Our pay was fourteen shillings a week, with a shilling a week for stoppages for the PSA (we never really knew what that stood for we nicknamed it Poor Sergeants Association) we were paid fortnightly and with being billeted at a holiday resort, you can imagine that by the end of the second week we were tight for money. There were all kinds of temptations to part us with our money, I was never broke but I was sailing close to the wind a few limes. Blackpool Pleasure Beach Co kept the Fun house open all year round. Servicemen were charged just sixpence and you could stay as long as you wished, the big snag there was that you hardly ever came out with the same cap overcoat and gloves, as you went in with. You see there was no attendant at the cloakroom .I did not go very often.

Blackpoll was where we got our first taste of RAF discipline, first of all we had to have our hair cut to regulation length. No hair had to be more than one and a half inches long, I had three haircuts in one day before I satisfied the sergeant. Having servicemen going back to the barber for another sliver to be cut off must have been rewarding. As we had to pay the barber ourselves, it did not happen to me again. Boots had to be polished until they glowed, the insteps had to be polished. Buttons had to be polished even at the back. Warrant Officer Sooty had a dentists mirror on a stick and he could see the our insteps with it

He was the first Warrant Officer I encountered and funnily enough he was the last I saw when I was demobbed. We where at Blackpool mostly to learn discipline, parade drill and marching, and P T, which for some was very badly required, they were in poor state. I would say that the Morse Code and Wireless procedure were our main subjects there. I knew the mores code before I joined up chiefly because our telephone system on the railway was based on it. I did have a go at it in the control office at Wakfiield Station even though I was not very fast at the beginning but it did help at Blackpool. We had our morse lessons in the old tram sheds at the back of the Coliseum Bus Station. In winter they were mighty cold and draughty, the first test was four words a minute, and if you failed you did not get another chance, then on to six eight ten twelve fourteen and sixteen a minute. At each stage up to twelve words a minute 'fail' mentt out. You see it was a long course to train to be a member of an air crew, and if you could not handle it then, it would be a waste of time and money if you failed later on. I can not remember how many failed in the early stages but probably quite a few. I do not remember anyone failing on the latter part of the course.

I do know that one of the lads who failed went on to be a pilot and he got to be a Squadron Leader

We did most of our square bashing and PT in Stanley Park, and on the promenade, weather permitting. I remember stripping into our P T kit and folding our clothes up and putting them on the snow. When the weather was inclement we would do our P T in the Tower Ballroom or the Empress Ballroom in the winter gardens. They were the finest ballrooms in Europe The floors were sprung and the care takers had to screw them down according to the number of people that were on, we were not allowed to jump more than nine inches.

Reggie Dixon was the resident organist at the Tower Ballroom and Reginald Porter Brown was the organist in the Empress Ball Room. Reggie Dixon joined the RAF and was made a Squadron Leader and never went out of Blackpool, he and Ralph Reader were in charge of forces entertainments in Blackpool, you see there were a hell of a lot of different services in the district, and the big wigs knew that moral had to be upheld.

We did our theory and procedure lessons in Rakes car show rooms in Church Street. One of our teachers had been the chief radio operator on the Queen Mary Liner. He also tried to teach us about Atoms Protons Neutrons and probably a lot of other (ons!) which I have long forgotten about.

At Blackpool we were lucky to have a shower once a fortnight. That had to be a quick affair because we had to go to Derby Baths for it, and there were such a lot of service personnel in the district they would be over whelmed. At times we must have smelled badly , what with having just one pair of trousers and the lack of bathing. I had a girlfriend there she was a lovely Geordie Lass, she would always pay her share of any thing we did. I did try my luck maybe the aforementioned BO put her off.

After about five, six months, we got seven days leave and were posted to No 2 Signal School at Yatesbury in Wiltshire. It was a peace time station with all the mod cons of the period, we were there to get up to eighteen words a minute in morse code. We were also taught a lot more about procedure and also had to be taught the Theory of Wireless and practical things , so that if there was a breakdown of our equipment when on ops we would have the rudiments of how to get them working again We were also introduced to different radio transmitters and receivers. The first set I used had a large box of coils and when you wanted to change frequency you had to put in a different coil and recalibrate the receiver and the transmitter. It was fiddly and could not be done quickly. However we soon went on to a lot better equipment The Marconi 1009 receiver and 1011 transmitter, it was a doodle compared to the other box of tricks, it had a magic eye which you could tune your receiver by. Then you could tune the receiver to the transmitter. We practiced a lot on these, they were not coupled to outside side aerial so you could not interfere with the outside world.

I enjoyed my time there, the huts were clean and dry, the food was pretty decent, and the weather was good. On the station there was a cinema where the films were changed twice a week. There were two good Naïf's, and one in particular used to occasionally make doughnuts. They were a real treat. There were also plenty of generous WAF' sand NAAFI girls.

I flew for the first time in a De Havilland Domini. a twin engine biplane and even today, around the world there are several still flying I thought that it was marvellous; I can still feel that thrill. Then we went on to Proctors single engine two seated monoplanes, pilot and WOP. I did my first live radio operating in them. While there we were kitted out with full flying regalia. We had all silk under wear, long stockings and gauntlets and boots. I never had to wear the flying gear, except for the boots, which were called escape boots. There was a small penknife in a pocket of one of the boots which enabled you to cut the tops off the boots and make them into shoes, if you were shot down, and you wanted to escape, you would look less conspicuous.

If we were abreast with our instructions, occasionally we were allowed to go camping. We slept in tents of course and did our own cooking, barbeques mostly. The corporal who was in charge must have been friendly with the Cookhouse Officer because we always had an abundance of food. A small river than through the campsite and we caught a fare few trout, do not ask me how because we did not have any fishing tackle, but they were very nice cooked in butter.

The only other time I have been camping was when I was in the boy scouts, we went to Oxspring Nr Penistone. We had to walk there a distance of about seven miles, taking all our kit and cooking equipment etc on a track cart. Which was propelled by britches arse steam, you would have thought that we were going abroad. Howard Walker was our Scout master; he eventually got to be District Commissioner. His family were the top dignitaries in our village, they very rightly commanded a lot of respect, they were the chief partners of the firm of, Bury and Walkers solicitors in Barnsley. They had beautiful extensive gardens and occasionally had garden parties moistly to raise funds to build a new Chapel in the village. Uncle Charles was their part time gardener he kept it in pristine condition; it was a credit to him.

On with me tale, I can only remember getting one seventy hour leave at Yatesbury it was too far to go home to Yorkshire, I would have only had time to say hello and goodbye. I was invited to one of my pals who lived in Weston Super Mare. His parents made me very welcome. So also did his girlfriend, she defiantly took a shine to me, and it was a bit embarrassing I am ashamed to say. I found it hard to resist because she was a stunner. I did make it with his sister, who was a very generous lass. Whilst there we went on a pub crawl, I imbibed a lot of 'Scrumpi' I can assure you it is not for learner drinkers, it's lethal.

At the end of the coarse we had a pretty stiff test, and I was pleased to have done well, forty per cent was a pass, I got sixty five per cent, and was put on for a further exam for promotion, passed that by the skin of my teeth (and a bit of help from a flight sergeant) and was promoted to the dizzy heights of AC1 previously I had been AC2. A shilling week extra. We were given our arm flashers to denote that we were fully fledged Wireless Operators.

The calamity struck we were stunned to hear that we were to be lent out to the Army, The Royal Signal Corps. Normally we would have gone for ground station experience. We were given seven days leave and told to report to Melbourne nr Pocklington in the East riding of Yorkshire. As it was rightly called then.

What a shock to the nervous and all other systems. We could not believe it, talk about primitive conditions, for us it was like going back to the

Stone Age. We were billeted in Nilsson Huts. All the beds were bunk beds with rough shoddy blankets probably from the Crimean war, no sheets. We were given paliasses and we did not know what they were. We were told to go down to the local farm and fill it with straw, creepy crawlies and all. We were told to shove as much as we could into it because it would compress. And it did, we had to go back a couple times before it became tolerable. That was to be our mattress, and for a while when you tuned over you were likely to get a straw up your rectum.

To say that we were down in the dumps was a bit of an understatement. The washing and sanitary arrangements were pretty awful and the food was grim. That can only be blamed on the cooks, because all food for the forces was distributed by the NAFFI and was the same for all three services, except for regional differences, foot instance if we were near a sausage factory we would get a fair share of there products. However we got our heads to gather and decided that had just make the best of it and get on with it, and take anything that they could throw at us. We were not to let the RAF down, so that evening we went into Pocklington to drown our sorrows and got nicely sizzled. I can assure you that falling out of a top bunk when you are inebriated, has a very sobering effect. Guess who it happened to.

Next morning on parade the Sergeant in charge noticed the shabby appearance of our uniforms and brought an officer to look at us. We explained that we only had got on what we had got. We were promptly taken down to the nearest Army Supply stores and we were issued with Army Battledress and fatigue dress. We looked a bit odd then, because we were allowed to keep our RAF forage caps, which as Aircrew trainees we were allowed wear a white flash in our caps. That was a bit confusing to the Army lads, because a white flash in an Army cap denotes that you are a trainee officer, Out of camp we regularly got saluted. It raised many a smile and also boosted our deflated ego's somewhat.

Then we got down to the nitty gritty next day we were put through the assault coarse it was a bit rough , but except for Henry Long a lad of half Chinese parentage, who was defiantly on the timid side, they tried to show us up epescially on route marching, when nearly every one had blisters on their feet. The same as before no one complained we just got on with it. Then we were tested to see how proficient we were at wireless theory and operating. Unfortunately. I did not do as well as previously , the equipment was unfamiliar, well that's my excuse.

I was allocated to be with a Corporal Sharatt. We had what was called an Ally Pall; don't ask me why, as far as I was concerned it was short for Crystal Palace a most unlikely comparison, it was a Morris Commercial lorry with a box fastened to it, that contained a transmitter and a receiver and all the ancillary tackle that went with it Sharratt was a pre war radio 'am, very competent and he had a boxful of gadgets to make the equipment work better. I learned a lot from him.

We were attached to the Dirty Dukes that of coarse is the Durham Light Infantry which was part of 55 Division. It was said that 55 divisions had been decimated in WW1 and would always be kept in this country. The ''truth?' well there did seem to be a lot old soldiers, in fact some of them had served all over the world. One who was called old Bill he was quite a character, the stories that he told could have filled a book. The last thing he took off at night after he got into bed was to take off his cap, and the first thing he did in morning before he got out of bed was put is cap on,, he said that he had been given 'jankers' for being caught without his cap on and he did not intend to be caught again.

We did not stay there very long before we moved to Fernley Park, Otley, Yorkshire. Could things get any worse? Oh Yes. We were billeted in Boer war tents that leaked like sieves. The washing and shower facilities were very primitive, cold water only for washing and shaving. We only got a shower when we had been on a route march, and that was in a sentry- type box, we were allowed just half a bucket of water each poured in through, like a sieve, on top. The toilets were a shed on wheels, with three compartments for doing you're thundering, the shed was over a trench, and when the trench was filled up it was wheeled on to a trench that had been previously dug. I'll bet there was some good celery grown there after the war. .

We did not stay there very long, shortly we moved to Weston park only about a mile away, winter was setting in by this time an eventually we were allowed to put three tents up inside a marquee, despite this it still rained in. In our tent we had acquired some large plant pots and some candles. We lit about four candles in one pot and placed another pot on top talk about central heating we thought that we had invented it seemed to make a difference. It was better than nowt!

I got friendly with a girl there. We clicked in Willy Woollies. Her name was Diana , she took me to her grandparents the first night, I was introduced to a lot of her relatives, got me feet under the table in quick sticks. After a couple of 'dates' she took me home and introduced me to her mother, her dad was a Sergeant Major farther and was abroad somewhere, 'thankfully' and her mother used to go to bed early, very obliging! Diana and I had one or two good times on her mother's settee. I really got my feet under the table there, I was invited to Sunday Tea a time or two. Remember that by now food rationing was really beginning to bite. I think if I had been stationed at Weston Park much longer, things would have escalated between us.

While there we went on a scheme to Scotland, it was code named 'Dry-shod' very appropriate, it peed It down for a fortnight,(I had heard that in Scotland there are only three seasons winter snow and midges) it was confirmed to me then. It was to emulate a landing in North Africa. I did not sleep in a bed for a fortnight. The best sleep we had was in a hay barn complete with creepy crawlies and micses. The scheme was a bit rough, quite a few were killed. The worst night was the last one, when I had to sleep on concrete garage floor with just one blanket. That was at Lockerbie where the air disaster occurred in 1988.

However, what do you think? We were on the move again once more we never went back to Otley we were the advance guard for us all to move to place called Little Levan between Beverley and Hornsey. We were billeted in a wood ,very complete with creepy crawlies. While there we bad an outbreak of scabies bought about by ditty blankets. Scabies is a litter insect that burrows under you skin. And I think the treatment for it was Ternosol Soap. With Gentian violet painted on, luckily I did not succumb to it. Those that did were not allowed out of camp, they looked like painted Red Indians, The nearest place for a drink was Beverley, about five miles away, Naturally we had to walk it there was no bus service. We used to frequent a small café just up the road which sold sandwiches and cakes. It was a nice cosy place with a piano. One of the lads was a decent piano player; we had some good old sing songs there. The owner was a lovely lady, who was like a mother to us. She had a buxom daughter who was about sixteen; I really had to take a hold on myself because she was coming on to me. I think because my pals took me you one side. I saw sense but I was sorely tempted.

Then, hey up what do you think? We were on the move once more (would you Christmas Eve it). This time to North Cave on the banks of the river Humber, we had to march there carrying full kit and a rifle, (and some kind of machine gun for part of the way) it must have been twenty miles. There were a lot of blistered fee. And a fair few had to drop out because of exhaustion. North Cave was a much improved camp than we had previously encountered, the food was also improved, so were the billets. There I was issued with my own rifle; it was a brand new Lee Enfield, 303 Calibre. I thought that I was a bit of a crack shot there. What I did not take into consideration was I was competing with a lot of squaddies who did not want to be good shots. They did not want to be sent to war, it was as simple as that! I would not like to say that the majorority were below par , but they were not the elite. It was obviously a very good rifle its sights were easy to calibrate, the sergeants used to borrow it .

While there I went greyhound racing a time or two with one of my pals who was the 'expert'. He seemed to know a bit about dogs, I knew nothing, we did not lose a lot. I do remember one race with a dog called Bally Hennessey again (be jay bus) running in it, my pal said we can put our shirts on this, it's a dead cert. thinly thing that was dead was our money, it had too much breakfast that day. It was leading the race when it got tangled up with its own feet and went arse over tit, so did our money.

About the 2nd December 1941 I went on seven days leave. Bessie and got permission to be married, I remember that at time we had to get her parents permission to marry because Bessie was only nineteen. We had to walk from Danby Dale to Kirkburton, six miles away to get a Special Licence we were married five days later at Upper Cumberworth Church. How it was managed I do not know. But it was a white wedding; both bridesmaids (Gladys and Anna) Bessie's Twin sisters were also in white. We had a proper reception in the band room on the Slade at Denby Dale. Food rationing was getting serious, by then, also clothing was rationed. Everyone rallied round and contributed something, talk about Dunkirk Spirit, it was nothing short of a miracle. We had two taxies; one brought my dad and me, Granma and Granddad and Auntie Nancy from Kexborough. That taxi was owned by Outran (the bus man) he stayed for the reception and took my relatives back home. It was convenient because he lived at Kexborough. My sister and family came. They lived at Silkstone about seen miles away. And had to get there by two buses, it must have been difficult for them. The other Taxi was hired from Hurst Bros who were also Haulage contractors in the village. By another stroke of luck my best friend was on leave at the time and was my best man. It was a uniformed wedding. We were both good-looking healthy lads (well if I can't blow me own trumpet who the hell can, especially in this story). Another big stroke of luck, the weather was lovely and fine. I cannot remember how I managed it, but I got my leave extended by a few cays.

When I got back to North Cave, I got a lot of leg pulling "Why have you done that you silly sod" and other flattering remarks. Then disaster struck. To my dismay someone had used my rifle and had not cleaned it properly, it had a rusty and pitied bore. I tried to clean it but to no avail I was at my wits end, it was a disaster to put it mildly. I tried to get to know which of the sergeants had used it, but they closed ranks! they knew nothing about it. After deliberating with my best friends, it was decided that I should hide the thing in the Ally Pally. It just fitted in behind the radio equipment I never saw it again. Luckily we did not all have riffles and I was able to borrow one when I needed to. How I got away with it god only knows.

You are not going to believe this!. Shortly after that we moved again. A big move this time in fact it was a colossal move. The whole division moved down to Truro in Cornwall. We had to travel by train, which was not a corridor train, it had no facilities whatsoever. Normally each compartment seated twelve persons; we had the luxury of just eight to a compartment. But we all had two kitbags each, and rifles, and all our webbing etc and a lot more bits and bobs so we were still cramped for space. We had to pee thought the window and be careful that some one nearer to he engine was not doing the same thing. A number two was more difficult, we had to do it on a piece of newspaper , and throw it out of the window always making sure that someone further down the train was not looking out. Not nice, but needs must. We were told that the train would stop frequently for refreshments and to stretch our limbs. However it only stopped occasionally, mostly in some sidings, we never knew where the hell were because all he station names had been taken down or blacked out. During the hostilities all names of towns and villages were removed, to confuse the Jerries if they invaded. I haven't a clue how people managed to get around after leaving there own localities, it must have been a nightmare, especially in the dark, and all road lighting was suspended. Lighting on vehicles was also much dimmed (hooded in fact).

The best stop was at Bristol Temple Mead Station. I had one of the best cups of tea inn my life there; it was (YES) out of a jam jar, absolute nectar! We had a meal and a drink there and the WVS were on hand to comfort us, and a padre was on hand to give us spiritual guidance. We hoped that he would give the train driver good guidance to get us to our destination as quickly as possible.

We eventually arrived at Truro and were billeted at a Country House called Trelawney House a famous Cornish name. It had been knocked about by pervious residents, but to us it was sheer luxury, after all our troubles. Much to our dismay we were to find that Red Caps were also billeted there. Red caps were the Army Police hated by every one. Next day our radio equipment arrived and immediately Corporal Sharratt set about contacting Divisional HQ in Yorkshire. We had to erect two aerial masts which were needed to transmit and receive at such a distance. He was very surprised when I knew how to do it, I had been trained to do this at Yatesbury, which at the time I thought, it would be difficult erecting an aerial mast as a radio operator when flying at 20,000ft. Just shows you, no education is wasted. We soon made contact, much to my dismay, However with help of one or two of Sharratts gadgets mind we got a good clear signal, I was a little disappointed I thought that we may be getting a day or two off from our duties. We operated from early morning until night. Then the Appleton Layer took over and dimmed our signals. I was on duty on Christmas Eve until the evening and I kept reducing power hoping that they would close me down, but someone must have rumbled what I was doing and promptly told me to stop it or I would be in serious trouble. You see I was anxious to be down in

Truro with me mates that were about two miles down the road. I think I broke the two minute mile that night. Once more I succumbed to his female attraction. I must explain that I never committed adultery. She was a nice Cornish lasso her name was June, she introduced me to her relations, I can't remember which, we got on nicely, and she had a very good job so she insisted that she paid for a lot of our entertainments.

On Christmas day those who could be spared from our duties were invited to local people's homes for Christmas dinner. They were lovely generous people, and we very much appreciated it, we also came away with a Christmas present.

Whilst at Truro we were sent out on an exercise called Initiative. We were taken out on a closed covered lorry and dumped in threes at various places in Cornwall. We just had our water bottles and emergency rations (hard tack what they were like I never found out) and an Ordinance Survey map. We had to find our own way back to camp. Think on, there were no signposts at that time. We were told that we had to act as if we were German agents. And must not ask any one for directions. The church towers and spires were a big help and the tombstones in the graveyards were very informative. There not all the village names had been obliterated. We got back alive and very hungry in decent time, we were praised by our officers for our inintiative; we all had to explain how we had done it. We were told before we set off that cheating would incur some punishment.

No, you will not believe it before you could say, "Jack Robinson" we were on the move again. How the hell did we 'win' the war, makes you wonder. This time it was to Tailstock in Devon. Once more we were in the middle of a wooded area. We arrived there at night, no lights on the roads of course. We were taken to out Nilsson huts and told where the cook house was, we were all starving by then. I set off by myself and almost at once I fell into a slit trench which was half full of, muddy water, bear in mind the soil down there is red, what a mess, I was lucky that I fell in feet first, otherwise I could have easily drowned. I had to shout for help, I was well and truly stuck; I went to the showers and got washed down without taking my cloths off...

Not very long after that we were repatriated to the RAF at Lords Cricket Ground, St Johns North. London. We were there mostly to be rehabilitated back into the RAF. We were billeted in so called luxury flats. Seymour House. (I was reminded recently about 'Lords' being used by the RAF during the war. When the Beautiful Lancaster did the combative fly past, I confess I shed a few tears.) The flats had been severely thrashed before we arrived, but were an improvement to some of our previous abodes. We had our meals at Regents Park Zoo, no not with the monkeys. We dined in the underground restaurant, and the food was exceptionally good. There were so many there that you could go round without chance of being caught. I remember one sergeant cook saying it's bloody marvellous when we have eggs for breakfast the population seems to double. We were there to be kitted out again. Luckily we were still carrying our chits which stated that we were entitled to another pair of trousers. So this is when we finally got them. Also as the RAF would not let us wear Army battledress we exchanged those for RAF battledress, which now meant that we had a grand total of three pairs of trousers; WOW then Geronimo arrived, we handed in our boots and were issued with shoes. Lovely.

Whilst there we went to the local bathing pool, where for the first time I learned to swim. Not very well but I was cuffed with myself. Also there we had ditching drills; we were given Mae West's and we had to jump fully clothed (we were give different clothing to wear) off a high diving board into the water, then we had to turn over an inverted rubber dinghy and climb into it. It was not easy but it would be more difficult in the open sea. Remember Henry Jong our timid comrade? What happened when it came his turn to jump off the diving board? Well he strode down the board as if full of confidence , reached the end , then slammed his brakes on just like the proverbial cartoon dog, after three attempts we shoved him off.. All aircraft were equipped with these dinghies, they saved many lives when planes had to ditch in the sea. Later on, some of the four engenend planes were issued with Lindholme Dinghies they were much better. The Dinghies carried radio transmitters that were cranked by a handle. They just sent out a continuous signal, which could be picked up by a direction- finding - equipment. They were also equipped with a box kite, which would carry an aerial. How the dickens you managed to fly a kite from a dinghy? Fortunately I never had to find out.

Whist there we went to a concert where two young ladies called Vera Lynn and Anne Shelton were singing If I remember properly, they both got to be a bit famous, they were of coarse "Forces Favourites" they were lovely. We were not long enough in London to explore all its delights. One thing really shook me, I was accosted by a lady of the night who assured me that she had the best Fanny in London, and I did not choose to explore that avenue. You see we had to have a FFI inspection every month. FFI means free from infection, mostly VD of coarse we of coarse called it Fit for Insertion. Also we had films about Venereal Diseases, the contents of which could put you off sex for life.

You will never believe this. We moved again. Back to No 2 Signals School at Yatesbury where we delved further into theory and procedure, whist there the Yankees had at last come into the war, previously we had used an X codes for our communications, now we had to use the international Q code These codes were to shorten messages, egg x259 was give me a bearing, now it was (I think) QDM. We soon got the hang of it I think QSA was " what is the barometric pressure at ground level" when we set off on long flights we knew what the barometric pressure was. On return it could have altered, the message back was a plus or minus number. Then we had to recalculate the altimeter which worked on the barometric pressure, this was all because we did not want the Germans to know what our weather conditions were.

Also there we were instructed on Air Gunnery and how to assemble and reassemble a Browning machine gun in semi darkness. We also had Aircraft recognition classes. One experiment I had to take part in was the theory that if you ate a lot of carrots, you would have better night vision. Our class was chosen for the experiment, and before it finished we were heartily sick and fed up of carrots. I am pretty sure that it was a lot of bullshit. We also did quite a lot of clay pigeon shooting. That was alright I really enjoyed that. I got quite proficient at it; it was to sharpen our reactions. A full box of cartridges came into my possession, which I took home next time I went on leave to exchange with the local farmer for some foodstuff's, eggs ,bacon, and milk were usually what I got. The cartridges were useful to him for shooting rabbits, hares and the odd pheasant that had 'strayed' onto his land. The cartridges were difficult for civilians to get. Later on the Squadron I could procure them very easily.

It was there that I managed to pass an exam in Morse code at twenty four words a minute. Which made me feel pretty chuffed with mesen! (Keep having to lapse into Board Yorkshire 'cos it's in me blood.

Well surprise surprise. we moved again, to Air Gunnery School at Porthcall in South Wales. We did not do any flying there , dummy aircraft went around on rails which meandered around quite a bit we were only simulating it seemed quite a farce to me. Signallers, as we were later called, we were only Emergency Air Gunners and only had to earn the rudiments of air gunnery. Duly we all passed out and received our Gunners badge, which had AG on it. Later it was changed to S for signaller. Then we got our stripes we were fully fledged Sergeants. And we all went on seven days leave. On this leave my first daughter was conceived. Much of my leave was spent showing off my new wing and stripes, to friends and relatives. I recall walking to Crigglestone to show to Bob Bishop and his wife, she thought a lot of me. He of coarse was my old Station Master, grand boss. I will relate to you a couple of his little adages, when I first worked with him on the railway, we had to share a desk, the desk had a line drawn down on it, and I was told never to trespass on his half. At the top of his half, he had etched the letters KBIS. I was quite a while before I dare ask him what it meant... He told me that it stood for was Keep Buggering in Steady. I have said it many times since. And tried to live up to it. On day he heard me saying, I can't do two jobs at once. He told me that he new of a lady who had done nine things at the same time. If you have a nervous disposition, turn away now. If not get someone else to read it for. You Ready

She sneezed---- coughed--- shit --- pissed --- and farted--- broke the pot

Cut her arse---spilled the piss----and spoiled the carpet.

He was quite a lad.

Then of coarse we were on the move again. This time to RAF Bridgenorth Salop. If I remember rightly, Bridgenorth was divided into high town and Low Town. The army had to keep to the High Town, and the

RAF had to keep to the Low Town. That was to stop fighting, you see we were not content to be at war with the jerries, we had to have inter service scraps just to keep our hand in. We were at RAF Bridgnorth to learn administration that was in case we were commissioned. Also we were instructed in the rudiments of navigation, we also had to keep our hand in at the morse code. And much to our dismay we had to do some square bashing. And on one occasion, much to our disgust a Corporal was in charge.

While there I developed a disorder in my right wrist, I could not tap out the "dashes and dots" well not at any speed. If it had not improved it would have been the end of my radio operating career. Thankfully the medics sorted it out for me. The food there was not up to our usual standards. Especially the dumplings. we seemed to got them every other day. You could have played cricket with them. We complained to the orderly officer, but things did not improve.

So we decided something drastic. It was almost as bad as treason. It was certainly a court martial offence. We decided on silent insubordination, it was only our section that took part. It was a big parade and our section did not respond to orders, we were threatened with very dire consequences. The CO was brought to us, a chap with a lot of scrambled egg on his cap. He dismissed the rest of the parade and then talked some sence into us; we aired our complaints about the food and he promised to look into it. Gave us a damned good telling off, we all had to do some extra fire patrols etc, the food in general did improve afterwards. Common since on that occasion did prevail. That is not a common thing in the services.

To our utmost delight we started to do the thing we had volunteered for. We were transferred to RAF Bobbington, sometimes called "Half Penny Green" to start flying. We flew in Anson aircraft, twin engines monoplanes. The Anson wasn't really made for wartime flying, but it was a very decent plane a workhorse in fact, we also flew in Oxfords a similar plane. A lot of experience was gained at Bobbington we also delved further into navigation. And were introduced to the vagaries of the Sextant. I do not think that many of us got the hang of that, me for one, fortunately we did not have to pass exams for it. I have never seen a Sexton since except on television.

As usual we did a great deal of morse practice and procedure, I must have greatly improved when sending on the morse key, because the instructor used to get me to do the sending for tests. To enable you to send at the required speed, a stop watch was used. I was very puffed up at that, only to be deflated at the end of the course. When in my Log Book was 'Air operating results-below stranded',I was rather surprised at that, because I thought I had done rather well.

Then we started the real thing, we were sent to RAF Silverstone No 17 Operating Training Unit. The first thing there was to Crew up, that meant putting 10 pilots,10 navigators, 10 bomb aimers. 10 radio operators, 20 gunners into a room together. The pilots chose the ones that they liked the look of then we left the room and went outside to introduce ourselves to each other, at the time I thought that it was a bit crude, but for us it worked. We got on like a house on fire. If the pilots chose on ability there would have been some motley crews.

When all these formalities were done we got down to the natty gritty of preparing for the real thing. First we were phographed in civilian clothes to take with us when went on those continental evening excursions. These were to put on identify cards by the resistance in France, for escape purposes. We all looked like escaped convicts. We were allowed two Benzedrine tablets; they were to suppose to pep you up and keep your wits about you, to give you a better chance to escape. Also a phial of Morphine in case we got injured. We were issued with Horlicks and Ovaltine tablets to give us a bit of sustenance and comfort. We had already been issued with emergency first aid kits at Padgate. Then we were introduced to the newest navigation aid which was called Gee. It was the newest radar aid and was a real improvement. We were sworn to secrecy. I will attempt to tell you how it worked, if you throw a pebble into a pond it creates ever increasing circles, if you throw three pebbles into a pond at exactly the same time you get lines formed from the intersecting circles, these form three straight lines , "that's the best I can do" these pulses were transmitted by radar and were picked up on a cathode ray tube onto time bases , these were calibrated on a special map and if it was done properly you could tell where you had been a few seconds previously. Before this navigation was done by dead reckoning, beacons and radio bearings, and map reading, this is ok when the weather is good, but not a lot of use at night. On the plane we had a loop aerial and we could take bearings from radio beacons, the later were not available over the continent.

Once more we had to up sticks and move again to Silverstone's Satellite Turwestern where we flew as a crew for the fist time. The Pilot was Sergeant Jack Petite, from London, Navigator Jack Peterson from Winnipeg, Bomb Aimer Barry Watts from Toronto, Rear Gunner was Robert Kerr from Alberta Mid Upper Gunner Leslie Major from Camborne in Cornwall, and of coarse himself Wireless Operator Mostly it was circuits and bumps and a little cross country flying, but no night flying. After about ten hours flying time it was decided that Sgt Petite was not suitable for heavy bombers and he was taken off and transferred to other duties. Then we had to start again with another Pilot, Roy Lake from Corydon. We called him 'puddle' he proved to be an excellent pilot, we all thought that it had been fate that things had turned out as they were. We were all thrilled to be back with Roy, you see he was our original pilot but due to an accident he had to go in hospital. All our activities were done as a crew, I am convinced that was the best thing we did. We were and acted as a pack.

Shortly after we crewed up, we decided to go for a ride to Buckingham on our bikes. We had not gone very far when Roy went arse over tit and split his head open; he was out for the count. We had to find a telephone to contact base to get him seen to, we all thought that he was a goner. He looked dreadful. However it had no permanent effect, except a couple of scars. It must have been written by the gods that he had to be our pilot. He rejoined us fourteen days later thank goodness I am sure that if we had stayed with Petite we would not have survived for very long. Unfortunately we had to endure the circuits and bumps once more but Roy was soon going solo. Whilst on these exercises my task was to contact, by radio as many other RAF stations as I could, I don't think I missed many. To enable me to do this we were given a book that contained all the call signs and frequencies of every RAF station in the British Isles.

The accident did not deter us, if you want to get about at these places you had to have a bike. These were plentiful on all airfields we liked to go into Banbury for the odd beverage, or 'five', medicinal of coarse. On one occasion I was so sozzled that it took me four or five attempts to get on my bike, I was getting on and off several times before I managed to stay on. However calamity struck once more. On the way back to camp the weather turned foggy and the pilot naturally! Who was in front, missed a corner and went straight through a Hawthorne hedge. His face and hands were a mass of blood and we thought "oh no not again , not another pilot, we got him back to camp to the sick quarters and got him seen to , things were not as bad as they looked they were only super facial scratches and he was fit to fly next day.

Near the end of the course I received a letter from my wife Bessie; she was in hospital with high blood pressure. I applied for compassionate leave and had to see the Commanding Officer. He looked at my records and saw that I had made more contacts than anyone else had ever done. And so allowed me a few days leave. Whilst on leave, the crew moved back to Silverstone, they took all my clobber with them. There we did a lot of cross country flying, practise bombing and some Fighter Affiliation; that was to give the gunners some firing "practice" and the pilot some experience of Corkscrewing. You do this to when being attacked by a fighter. It is difficult to describe this manoeuvre, but as the name suggests. It is like flying about the sky like a corkscrew. It was always a bit hairy, and you get a fair bit of G, (that's gravity pull) if it was done with proper timing it made it very difficult for a fighter to get a shot at you. On many occasions when we were on our evening excursions, when we had one or two hair-raising events! It proved very useful. On one of the first flights at Silverstone, we lost an engine just after take off. We were told to jettison a lot of our fuel before landing, in case we crashed.(Why?) We found out later that evening in Towester, that it had caused quite a scare. On another occasion whist flying over the Wash in Norfolk we were stuck by lightning. We thought we were being shot at by our anti- aircraft guns. We landed at the nearest airfield to be checked out. Luckily for us it was a Yankee airfield and we were treated like royalty, they did us proud. What a difference between our food and theirs. We had a very good meal with the extra special treat of some ice cream. This was something that we had nearly forgotten about. The pampering did not last long. We discovered that the only damage we had suffered was to my trailing aerial which had been burnt off by the lightning. It was as if it had been welded at the end. We had two aerials; one fixed to a mast just behind the Astor dome to the rudder, the other was the trailing aerial which was a long wire with lead weights on the end that had to be let out on a reel. I had to be careful with this it had a brake on to stop it flying out into space. But if I lost one it, I had to pay a fine of five pounds.

Later on, in Lancaster's we had a double fixed aerial on to each of the two rudders. I never used the trailing aerial, I and others thought it was a potential hazard to our own aircraft, imagine one getting caught around the propeller shaft it could have been catastrophic

Our local watering place was Towester (toaster as it was called) we had some good times there they were very friendly people, once more I fell for the female attraction, I'll just name her as Rosie. She was a married woman; her husband was a soldier. Shame on both of us. (Yes I do feel very ashamed of myself now) but it was war time and things _were different then!_ No we did not copulate!! But I was sorely tempted. We never went out separate ways from the others. Roy was consorting with her sister, we went to the local pubs and dances and cinemas together I also had a girlfriend on the base TUT TUT I know that it was abominable, but even before I went on operations, flying was a bit dicey the planes we flew to practice on, were planes that had been taken off operations.. We were at Silverstone for about four months, it had been quite enjoyable. That was the end of the course, we went on leave for ten days after which we had to report to RAF Scampton near Lincoln. We did no flying there it was very boring. Scampton was being used as a holding station. While its runways were being improved, I think we were there because there was a shortage of operational planes, we were only there a few days, it was Christmas time so they sent us on leave for seven days, very nice. While I was at home my first daughter Sandra was born.

About the end of January we were posted to RAF Wigsely about ten miles away. That was a Heavy Conversion Unit, where our pilot was commissioned his rank was Pilot Officer; also at that time we were to acquire an Engineer. His name was Robert Baird and he hailed from Morpheth in Northumberland we called him Geordie he had a distinct Geordie accent.

We were now flying four engined Short Stirling Bombers ,with Hercules sleeve valve engines to me they were great big cumbersome things a bit like big crows, I did not like them the important thing was that the pilot took to them ducks to water, going solo in about three and a half hours. My Equipment was exactly the same. Unfortunately we had to endure circuits and bumps again. Geordie was a bit green he was straight from Engineers School and had never flown before. It must have been a hell of a shock to him, he was only nineteen. On the first flight as we just got airborne, he noticed one if the engines were over heating and he said in a very excitable Geordie Accent -- Feather the port outer immediately -the pilot had very little experience with this aircraft and it could have caused us to crash. Fortunately the pilot ignored it and when we got to a decent height he throttled back and the overheating problem was solved, and it never happened again. He was a grand lad and tuned out to be a god engineer, and a valuable crew member. The Stirlings were quite often out of order, magdrop was usually the problem (magneto drop lowers the efficiency of the engine) I think? You see same as the Wellingtons they were clapped out planes that had been taken off operations... We were glad to get away from there and were delighted to be told we were going to RAF Silverstone No5 Lancaster Flying School We were now flying in the beautiful Lancaster, the thougabred of the bombers it was lovely to look at and easy to fly, it was very well equipped and extremely reliable. I did a lot of flying hours in the Lancaster and we only had to stop an engine on one occasion and that was because it had been damaged by a fighter. I compare the Wellington Stirling and Halifax to the Lancaster as comparing a crow to a swallow.

Don't tell me I was lucky I know bloody well I was, not many days have gone by since the war when I have said so to myself. One of my quirks is, going to the mirror in a morning and if I cloud it when I breathe on it, then I know that I have cracked it for that day. I have fooled the devil once more; I am just getting on with it. Less of the hilarity now George - we are now coming to the serious side of things. Syerstone was only a short course about twelve hours flying time there. Lots of lectures had to be attended concerning our future flying on operations; this was the last place to learn. Next lot would be all for real.

We were then posted to RAF Bardney near Lincoln it was a satellite of RAF Waddington. Which is still a very important RAF station? Now we were really at war. No 9 Squadron is one of the oldest in the RAF it was and still is one of the most respected Squadrons, we operated with 617 squadron (the dam busters) when they required some more weight. They *were* the elite, no doubt about that. Some of their operations were nothing short of miraculous. They were crewed mostly by second tour air crews. That means the crews especially the pilots had done at least one tour of thirty operations. I met some of these individuals later; at RAF Finningley many of them had shot nerves.

In the first five days there we did about fifteen hours flying time, all non operationonal. Then the streaky- underpants stuff started. The first op was to Toulouse in Southern France. Nine hours flying time. Apart from flying through two thunderstorms and plenty of flak, it was a piece of cake. (Well we were still alive)I was only a bit scared (said he) as I have said previously we just had to get on with it.

The next was a different story .It was one of the worst. It was to Mainly- Le- Camp just south of Paris 'I think'. There were four divisions of Panzers stationed there; the most feared tank of the war. They were centrally positioned to pounce wherever we were to land on D Day. The Germans new that the time was getting near. Squadron Leader Willy Tate briefed us for that raid. He said now then chaps, tonight it's not the usual women and children that we are to bomb to night, it's the real thing. He explained that the time of the bombing was calculated for when the maximum of men would be back on camp. So that all the soldiers would be back from the pubs, wheelhouses and brothels. We were to bomb at eleven thirty at night and completely obliterate the place. However there was a great loss of life on our side, a lot of our planes were shot down The wonderful (and I sincerely mean this) Lenard Cheshire VC was the Master of Ceremonies on that occasion and he kept us flying around the target for twenty minutes, on that occasion he was flying very low in a Mustang P51 Fighter plane. Actually it was the fist time he had flown in that kind of plane. He would not let us bomb the target until it had been market properly. Marking was done by Pathfinders they dropped different coloured markers that would burn for a long time. And then after he was satisfied, that target had been properly marked, hr let us bomb. We were flying upwards of Eighteen Thousand feet. I am sure that some of the losses were due to mid air collisions. Imagine three hundred large planes flying in a tight area probably some on right hand curcuits and some on left hand circuits it wasn't ideal. Nothing had been said at briefing about this situation arising. In the RAF records there were Thirty Missing, I think it was a hell of more than that. You see while we ere doodling about for twenty minutes the German fighter planes had plenty of time to get to us. Think on that each Lancaster or Halifax plane had a crew of at least seven, a lot of valuable lives were lost. But it must have reduced casualties on the invasion front. Four Panzer Divisions would have caused a lot more casualties.

Altogether I did forty operations that counted - about half to Germany, half to France. Twenty five were night raids and the remainder were daytime ones. At night we were to see firework displays the likes of which would have shamed any displays I have ever seen, especially in the Ruhr Valley It was like flying through hell, we used to think how the hell are we going to get through that lot. Day light raids were different you see at night you saw the flash and it was gone , in the day time , you would seethe flash and then the little black cloud that stayed , I used to think the black spots will fill in and so shall we. On daylight raids we were well looked after by Mustang P51 fighters, we hardly ever saw them.

I will only highlight a few ops that stand out in my mind. One was to Rennes in south West France, were we the target was a pyrotechnic factory. It is probable that it was something else of more importance as well. However we did see firework display better than the Yanks put on for Independence Day. We suffered some flak damage on that occasion, nothing serious. Because of fog at base,we were diverted to Turnery on the west coast of Scotland. When we arrived there the cloud base was very low. It was decided that we should break cloud over the sea. The navigator told the pilot what coarse to take, when we eventually broke cloud we saw some rock directly beneath us, the air was blue between pilot and navigator! Like you told me we were over the sea. We climed again and saw what happened and when we finally broke cloud we saw what happened, we had previously broken cloud directly over the island of Alias Craig. Peace reigned once more between pilot and navigator. However, that was not to the end of our troubles. When we came in to land the under carriage warning light cam on, that denoted that the undercarriage was not locked down. We flew round again and we thought that we had lost some hydraulic fluid due to flak damage. So we decided to top it up from the 'pee can' which was used by the forward crew to relieve themselves. We had an Elson toilet somewhere at the rear of the plane; as far as I know it was never used. However this procedure did not make any difference. By now we were getting very low on fuel, we just had to land. We were told by control to land on the grass at the side of the runway. Two fire engines and an Ambulance were waiting for us to land in case we crashed; we landed quite safely, the warning light must have been on the blink.

Turnberry was a very small station and they must have been very stretched to deal with us, there must have been ninety NCOs' and fifty officers, our crew and some others had to stay there a couple of days for repairs. That evening in the small sergeants mess there was a dance and the Wafts and local girls were invited, with extra crews there we supped them out of beer in quick sticks, and then turned our attentions to the short stuff By the way we were not allowed to take any money on operations with us so we had to go to the pay office to get a loan other wise we would have been out in the cold. Apparently I was so sozzled that I tried to dance with the Station Warrant officer, who on all RAT stations is God. Next morning when I awoke, fully clothed with even with my shoes on, a head full hammers that were trying to compete with each other, and a mouth like the bottom of a parrots cage I heard the tannoy announcing " Will Sergeant Parkinson report to the SWO's office." Apparently he was not amused with my conduct the previous evening and asked me to apologise for my behaviour, this I refused to do , so he took me to the Co's office explaining what my behaviour had been like. The Co dismissed the Station Warrant Officer. and then said to me, now you know that the SWO 'whose position I must recognise at all times' had never flown in his life, so he could not under stand the stupid things that Operating Air Crew's got up to I could consider myself admonished., it would not go any father than his office. But if I found myself in front of him again I would find myself in serious trouble. We soon ran out of money so I did not have the opportunity to make a fool out of myself again. Well not there!

Another very dicey excursion was to Prouville, northern France to bomb some caves where Buzz Bombs were stored These were Flying Bombs; very crude to look at but very effective, they were basically a Jet Bomber that was just a flying fuselage; no pilot; filled with explosive which was launched from a ramp, with enough fuel to reach its destination. When the engine stopped it fell like a stone. London was the principle target; they caused a lot of damage. Fighter planes dare not shoot them down because of the blast from the bomb, but they used to fly at the side of them and tip their wing to flip them over, that upset the Giro which acted as an automatic pilot, they were mostly shot down over the sea. But the majority got through. This was Hitler's first secret weapon. Worse were to follow.

On the way back from Prouville, we were coned by about twenty four searchlights, I can assure you when that occurs you feel as if everyone on the earth is looking at you. Fortunatly at that time we were using a devise called Monica, which was my responsibility to operate. It was a Radar devise operated by a cathode ray tube. I will try to describe how it worked. On the tube was a line called the time base; the line was across the middle of the tube. When we first took off, on each trip, the engineer would call out to me, what height we were in hundreds of feet I had to mark the tube with a yellow china graph pencil, when another aircraft came up to us (behind only) a blip appeared on the tube denoting how far away it was. By the shape of the blip I could see whether it was above or below us. Please forgive my rambling explanation; well it was over sixty years ago.

However, every one, especially the gunners was blinded, so my expertise came into force then. I could see, on Monica, a blip coming up very fast, and when it got to shooting distance, about three hundred yards I told the pilot to Corkscrew to port immediately We then had a very hairy time, which seemed like a month before the pilot managed to escape from the searchlights. We had been attacked by Three JU88 which was very formidable fighters. The gunners had managed to shoot one down and damaged another. The third buggared off to find an easier prey. We had suffered some damage but no blood was let. The starboard inner engine was running very rough, so it was feathered, if not it would have acted like a windmill and would have slowed us down. The Lancaster will fly easily on three engines. So that was not a problem. It was only when we got back to base that we realised how fortunate we had been. A hole had been bored through one of the propeller blades. As if by a machine. That was the explanation for the engine running rough. We also had a hell of a lot of small hoboes in the starboard wing. However we were all unscathed; the pilot was awarded the DFC for that op, to tell the truth I was a bit miffed because I dud not get even a mention.

Believe me there were no 'easy' ops' there was always some silly sod below or up above that were taking pot shots at us, I mean well it wasn't cricket was it ,we were only merely dropping bombs on them after all. It was that kind of humour that allowed us to 'get on with it.

Another very memorable op was to Leipzig in Easy Germany. It was the weather men that gave us the wrong information. They told us there would be two alters of cloud and we should fly between them. Unfortunately there was only one layer of cloud, and it was a bright moonlit night. So if we flew on top of the cloud we would be silhouetted and would show up like sitting ducks. If we flew in the cloud we would 'ice' up. If we flew below the cloud e would be caught up in the searchlights and clobbered by the Ack Ack. We did manage to get to the target, but unfortunately the losses were considerable. On the way back we were to experience another 'streaky pants' situation. We were we thought that we were in the comparative safety of the North Sea. When the pilot decided to have a pee, he had to get out of his seat to do this. So he engaged 'George' the automatic pilot. As he was peeing the Giro that controls George toppled, this caused us to go into a very steep dive. The pilot had a helluva job to get back to his seat. It took him and the engineer all their combined strength to pull us out of the dive. We thought that we were going to 'buy it. That however was not the end of our problems. The pee can was an oil can and of coarse the top was off and the contents emptied over the navigator and his equipment and charts, also it bad put 'Gee' out of order. Luckily my radio was unscathed and managed to get us bearing and a fix, so we managed to get back to base. No other damage was sustained to the plane. To use an RAF saying, 'we had been pissed on **at** a great height.'

Of course we had many other dicey escapades After D Day the port of Brest was out on a limb for a while, it was isolated We went there two days in succession. The first time we were only shot at lightly. We thought that they were running out of ammunition. So next day we went in a bit lower, and they shot the shit out of us, these were daylight raids. We got away with it a fair few didn't, I can tell you it is not pleasant seeing your comrades 'buying it'.

Coming back from that op I did something I had never done before on operations I tuned in to the BBC forces programme and let the rest of the crew listen to it. It could have had serious consequences; you see I had to listen out to base for messages every quarter of an hour, and I missed one 'the only one I ever missed' which was informing us that the Barrage Balloons were up at Yeovil. We only missed them by the skin of our teeth! Base call sign was NR8 and 5 groups were 9SY. Group transmitter was very powerful I think you would have heard it all round the earth. When there was a message they would just send out a number which I had to record in my logbook. I had to do a crafty one then, I left a space in my logbook and as soon as we landed I collared one of the other Wops so that I could fill in the missing message. Jammy once more, I prefer to call it imitative.

By this time the Bomb Aimer and I were promoted to Flight Sergeants and the pilot to Flight Lieutenant and the navigator commissioned. The Pilot was now Commanding Officer B flight. By this time he was the seventh Flight Commander whilst I had been on the station. It worked out one a month. I think that illustrates the causalities.

Another trip was to Flushing on the Dutch Coast. It was rumoured that it was lightly defended; we were to goon ahead to find 'a wind' to do this we had to drop smoke markers in the sea and take note of the drift... it was the task of the navigator and the bomb aimer to do this. The pot shooters on the ground left us alone the first time round. However on the next round they had the cheek to try to blow us out of the sky. Can you believe it? The bomb aimer said I think this job is a bit dangerous!

One after noon , all the air crews on the base were taken to Woodhull Spa the home of the Dambusters,we were there to e told that we were on cfor a coarse for a top secret operation , if we valued our lives we were not to tell anyone about it. On the way there our bomb aimer guessed what the target would be. We were going there to be briefed for the bombing to the Battleship Turpiz in a fiord in Northern Norway. Mr Churchill had sent for Bomber Harris and told him that at all cost the Tirpitz had to be taken out , it was tying up too many ships of the Navy, in case if broke out. Many different operations had been tried before with no success. Bomber Harries said he was confident that the Dambusters would do the job with the help of 9 Squadron.

Because it was too far away to bomb it from this Country we were to fly to Archangel in North Russia, refuel and wait for suitable weather, at the Fiord, and attack it from there. There were big problems to be solved Lancaster's were only designed to fly a maximum of ten hours, the journey to Archangel was twelve hours, modifies had to be done. The Mid Upper and front turrets were removed and all armour plating was removed. And extra fuel tanks were put in the fuselage. Also on the perimeter just before take off the tanks were topped up. Things were so tight.

We were to carry Tallboy Bombs twelve thousand ponders. And part of 617 was to carry some special kind of mines.

It was announced at the briefing that Wing Commander Lenard Cheshire had been awarded the VC. The place rocked with the applause, he had done over one hundred wartime operations, some of them being extremely hazardous. He was not awarded the Victoria Cross for any specific operation, it was for constant valour over a sustained period, I did not have the pleasure of meeting him, but he was practically worshipped on his Squadron. After the war he set up the Cheshire Homes, unfortunately a lot of them are now closed. But the Cheshire Foundation is still going strong. I strongly recommend you to read his story. It was published in about 2000, reading it was very emotional to me. He was an extraordinary man, he married Sue Ryder in 1959, they later became Baron and Baroness Cheshire they received a Variety Club's Humanitarian Award in 1975. in the House of Lords Lady Warsaw as she was known , was involved with debates about defence, drug abuse, housing, medical services unemployment and race relations.

The Queen Mother Opened the Sue Rider Foundation At Cavendish in 1979.

Back to my story, once more a little mishap occurred. On the evening of September11th we set of to go to Archangel carrying a twelve thousand Tallboy Bomb and a hell at lot of fuel,it was about a twelve hour flight most of the squadron was equipped with new planes - mark 10 Lancaster's and we all had some new improved bomb sights. Which were considerably better than the previous ones? However as we were turning on to the runway I thought that I felt the pane judder, I mentioned this to the pilot, he said that it was probably the tail wheel shimmying, which happened occasionally.

With that kind of a load on it took the full length of the runway for us to take off. We were now in line with our 'drinking clinic'. The Railway Hotel in Bardney Village. We had been stationed there for a considerable length of time, we had become regulars and the pilot used to waggle his wings a bit on take-off as if to demonstrate "look its us we are off on our evening excursions again". We climbed slowly and I started to feel a bit chilly which was very unusual for me. Where I was ensconced was the warmest part of the plane. I mentioned it to the pilot and he said, "stop moaning parky" However I got colder and was beginning to think that when we reached twenty thousand feet I was going to be frozen. You see I never wore any of the flying suits and silks that had been issued to me at Yatesbury. I could no longer contain myself. I had an inspection cover at the side of me and I could see into the bomb bay, I took it off, cast my eyes downwards and found out why I was so cold. The bomb doors were open quite a considerable distance. I immediately informed the pilot about this , we were now over the middle of Kingston On Humber.The pilot said to the bomb aimer "Have a look down in the bomb bay to see what the grumpy sod is on about" The bomb Aimer who was a French Canadian, said to the pilot "don't do any thing drastic right now because the bomb could drop off any second." The bomb was fastened by an electrically operated sling on the thickest part of its body and the sling had slipped to within a foot from its end. That is what had caused the bomb doors to be open, that must have been the judder I had felt… we had a crew discussion as to we should do, we could go back to base , which was too risky, we could go back over land, head it out to sea on automatic pilot and bale out. Nobody fancied that. Or we could head out over the sea and dump it. we chose the latter, we then had to climb to a safe height bearing in mind that if you are too low, and that size of bomb exploded, (we were supposed to drop them safe) the blast could be life threatening not only to those around the target, but also to the crew who dropped it When we got to a safe height over the North sea, the Bomb Aimer pressed the button to release the bomb! Nothing happened. Things were starting to look a bit grim. We had another Paw-wow and it was to put the plane into a shallow dive and try again. Nothing happened, now things were not at all rosy. So it was decided to put it into a steep dive and try once more. To our relief it worked and we returned to base to be met by Group Commander Sir Ralph Cocranane who of course wanted to know all the details. I think he was a bit sceptical until he heard about the damage that the plane had suffered. Also we realised just how lucky we had been. When the sling had slipped the bomb had slipped back so that its fins were stuck in the fuselage very close to the extra fuel tanks, However we found out if the bomb had been released, first time it would have taken the back half of the plane with it. And that would have curtains for all of the crew, nobody would have had a clue what had happened. The plane had to go for major repair as the fuselage was wrinkled.

Another remarkable op was to the Sorpe Dam ay the southern end of the Ruhr Valley the Dambusters had failed to breach this one. It was a daylight raid just involving our squadron, twenty planes in total. We were caring twelve thousand Tallboy bombs. I must point out at the moment of release when dropping these bombs, it seemed as though you are ascending in an express lift.

On this trip I was chosen to send back the message to say whether or not we had breached the dam. This boosted my ego some what. I had been given a crystal to tune the transmitter with, but I did not use it I was confident that I could do it without. However due to the structure of the dam like the Dambusters, we also failed to breach it... I had to send back the message 'failed to breach' it was very disappointing. Because several of our bombs went extremely close to the target. Several years later the Germans were still digging out a couple of the bombs which had not exploded. On this occasion we were protected by the trusty

Mustang fighters which were rarely apparent. We had been assured that we would be well looked after, but we were well pestered by the Ack Ack. However by that period of the war the Luftwaffe did not have the same strength as they previously had. Another thing in our favour was that the Yankees were on a raid well north of us. Luckily for us the Luftwaffe had bigger fish to fry.

To while away the time whilst waiting to take off on some excursions, we played cricket with other crews and the ground staff We also played Knur and Spiel a Yorkshire game that was played with a stick for the spiel and a big white potty (that is a large marble) for the knur. The potty had to be balanced on a piece of wood. The other end of the wood was tapped with the spiel thus popping the potty up in the air, and then you had to hit the potty with the spiel, these were good for the eye to hand coordination. We also played Crown ad Anchor. Though I have not the faintest idea how to play it now. Various card games helped to while away the time.

After we had done thirty operations were entitled to have a rest, perhaps go on refresher courses or go to training units. We chose to stay on the Squadron (quite mad) and go on operating. Except for the upper gunner Les Major he chose to go on non operating duties. We then picked up a new upper gunner. Mucker Morton a 'Brumbie' quite a character, he was a very good cartoonist, he had been badly burned on a previous operation he had significant facial scarring. On one operation to the Normandy Coast whilst taking off, halfway down the runway the engineer noticed that the airspeed indicator was not working. Brakes were slammed on and we came to a halt in the grass on the edge of the airfield. Nobody was hurt. Without the airspeed indicator one can not navigate. The pilot was having a fit; he thought that he had not removed the Pitohead cover. This was the part of the instrument which indicated the airspeed, and it was his responsibility to se that it was removed. However, this was not the cause of the problem. We had hardly come to a halt when the crew bus arrived to take us to a spare aircraft.

Squadron leader Harry Pooley ushered us to another plane and told us to hurry up to catch up with the others. Muckers reaction was "Mr Pooley we are not going any where until I have drawn Mr Chad (in chalk) on the fuselage" ask your granddad what Mr Chad was. Mucker would never fly in any aircraft without first drawing Mr Chad on it. Nearly all aircrew had superstitions of some sort. Except me of course, I had only a few teeny ones such as putting a sock on inside out, of coarse it was too much trouble to take it off again. Also before each excursion I would polish my shoes and my cap badge I thought that if my top and toes were clean and shiny providence would attend to the bits in between, Geordie liked to play snooker just before we set out. Our bomb aimer who was rather over- sexed. And was always boasting of his conquests. He fancied a 'lady' who every one always refered to her as "Aircrew Annie" She was one of the civvies that worked on the station, she was rather liberal with her affections. It was noticed that the lads who had succumbed to her delights soon 'bought it' (by the way no one was referred to as being killed or missing they had bought it) Soon after one evening in the pub Barry was paying too much attention to this 'lady' we took him to one side and told him to 'cut it out 'or we would 'cut them off'. So far as I know he heeded our advice.

On of the rear gunners, who was a veteran of about twenty operations must have had a very warped since of humour. He would approach any new crews on the station, he would approach them like the proverbial spiv " saying 'Pist- would you like a squadron tie" Usually the answer would be in the affirmative. He would whip out a pair of scissors and quickly snip off the end of their tie saying " there you have one now!"

About this time all air crews were issued with Colt thirty eight calibre revolvers and six rounds of ammunition that had to be accounted for. The powers that be were very stringent about this. However we discovered that stem gun ammunition had the same calibre and that was more freely available. This enabled us to have a bit of fun, and play cowboys and Indians, tin cans were plonked on railing tops so we could take pot shots at them. It was almost as dangerous as going to war. One evening after returning from the 'drinking clinic', there was a rat in the Nilsson hut, so Mucker took a pot shot at it. As the huts were constructed of corrugated steel, with concrete floors, the bullet ricocheted around the hut. You have never seen chaps diving under beds as quick in your life. The big wigs in there 'wisdom'. So how dangerous it was, and took them away from us. Why on earth they were issued in the first place the lord only knows.

I have always admired the courage of the American Air Force air crews. They suffered terrible casualties; they went deep into Germany without any fighter cover for protection on day light raids. That was when the Luftwaffe was at full strength. I'm glad I was not with them. We were awful with them we used to rib them quite a lot, singing to the tune of John Browns Body Lies a Moulding in the Grave, the following ditty.

You are flying Fortresses at thirty thousand feet
Ditto
Ditto.
But you've only got a teeny weeny bomb
Bags of guns and ammunition
Ditto
Ditto
And it only makes a teeny weeny hole.
We are flying Avro Lancasters at twenty thousand feet
Ditto
Ditto
But we carry a bloody big bomb
Glory Glory when we drop it
Ditto
Ditto
It makes a bloody great hole.
Some times a little private war went on between us.

Around this time there as a position on the Squadron for an Air Sea Rescue Officer. The Signals Officer recommended me for a commission so I could fill the vacancy. I had to go before the Squadron Commanding Officer, Wing Commander Bazin, who I did not like, I had flown with him on a couple of ops. Instead of the crew using Christian names on ops, with him we had to be prim and proper. For example, over the intercom we had to say "Wop to Pilot" and such like instead of the usual banter that went on between our crew. I think I did not put my case as well as I could have, any how he did not recommend me for a commission. I could have appealed to the Station Commander but I did not follow that course. I was a little disappointed and let down. I had seen people who had been commissioned that in my opinion who were defiantly below par. but you see it would have been an Irish mans rise of pay. For the first year I would have been worse off financially, I will explain .The RAF provided the initial uniform, after which officers then officers had to purchase their clothes. Puss the mess fees had to be paid. Which could be very heavy on the pocket. Until this time I had no doubt that my ability would get me through theses silly games, I would think that a lot more thousands had the same attitude. I now began to think "this war game is getting bloody dangerous" we did not seem to be going on all the ops that the rest of the Squadron were going on, hanging about is not in my system I want to get on with it. The ones we were going on seemed to be the 'dicey' ones.

The Bomb aimer, the Rear Gunner and I decided that we would like to be taken off operational duties, we had had enough. We had to go before Wing Commander Bazin, if I said he was accommodating I would be lying he threatened to put LMF 'Lack of moral fibre' on our records. We objected bitterly too this remark. And asked to see the Group Commander. CO of the station. He asked us to reconsider our decision, and gave us a couple of days to think about it. When he then saw us, he new we were series about it, and he spoke to us like a father and assured us that no mention of LMF would be put on our records. He said that we had done far more than the statutory number of operations and we could hold our heads up and look anyone in the face.

The Bomb Aimer and the rear gunner went back yo Canada. And I was sent to Bomber Command Instructor School at Finningley Nr Doncaster. this meant that I was a lot near home. I had not been there very long and I was promoted to Warrant Officer I was ' asked' nay told that to do the job of looking after the Reference Library. The job was very boring, so after being a runner, which was taking messages from one department to another I asked to go back on flying duties. The amount of ribbing that I had to take while I was doing the runners job, contributed heavily to my decision. When I was promoted to Warrant Officer I was kitted out with a much better dress uniform. It was almost like an Officers uniform; I thought that I looked the bee's knees n it. The fabric was of much better quality than I previously had been wearing it was similar to Barathea the only garment that I did not like was the greatcoat to my mind, it did not match up to the rest of the uniform, by devious means I managed to acquire enough clothing coupons to buy a Gabardine raincoat. Don't ask me why, but we were not allowed to wear Warrant Officers insignia on raincoats. The Royal Coat of Arms was the insignia. This caused confusion, my appearance was exactly the same as officers so I was saluted quite a lot, and I never succumbed to retuning the salute that would have been wrong.

While there we were allowed to do quite a bit of clay-pigeon shooting, which meant that the prohibited cartridges became available again. This resulted in more bargaining power with the farmers. Another very good perk while on operations we were allowed on each operation a bar of chocolate some Horlicks and Ovaltine sweets, and a small can of pure orange juice, (and I mean 'pure')

At Finningley, we were allowed all the same goodies on each flight we made, and we flew twice a day some times I used to go home with an attaché case full of these delights, which made me extremely popular with my friends and relations, and my illicit activities. You see these things were strictly rationed in Chivvy Street, well I **was** doing a pretty dicey job, well that's my excuse...

Also, on the operational squadron, we were allowed seven days leave every six weeks, unfortunately, a lot never survived to benefit from even there first consignment of leave. Much to my surprise, at Finningly, we still qualified for the same leave. Compared to operations it was a dodle but not without its scary moments, we used to do pretty dicey things at times, like practicing stalling, corkscrew flying, flying on two engines, and on one occasion with Wing commander Thompson on one engine This was on the First of the Battle of Britain anniversaries. That was juggling with Jesus a little too much. My room mate bought it, flying on one engine in a Wellington aircraft. But guess what I am going to say now? 'We just had to get on with it'.

I used to like going on Beacon Duties, it was similar to a lighthouse, it flashed out the first and last letters of which ever station you were on, in our case it was FY, they only flashed in the hours of darkness. The following twenty four hours after you had been on that duty, you were off duty. At that time I could be home in Danby Dale before ten o'clock in the morning. The chief reason I liked Beacon duties was that we were allowed enough food to feed a small Army. There was a caravan with the

Beacon with cooking facilities but of coarse no sleeping facilities. The Beacon was operated by a diesel engine. One other air man was with me, an engineer. When the airman had taken what he wanted, from the food supply. I would leg it home at great speed with the reminder. It was greatly appreciated. The food consisted of Bread butter, bacon eggs sausage, liver and some cooked meat, not all of these at the came time. Also from time to time I would get my mess tin filled with pork dripping. You can bet I was very popular with my in laws. I would do my utmost to get extra beacon duties by swapping with lads who could get home as easily as I could. If I could, I would hitch -hike home, I was not very often I had to pay the fare on a bus, I knew the majority of the conductors and drivers. (Most of them were women) they used to save tickets to show to inspectors who may get on the bus.

I shall never forget VE day. Almost every one on the station was allowed three days leave. I remember that I went down to the bridge at Doncaster trying to thumb a lift, when an old battered Austin Seven car cane along with two sailors in it, I thought "never look a gift horse in the mouth" so I got in with them, but straight away I thought "watt the hell have I done now" they were both sloshed to the eyebrows and the driver was meandering all over the road. When we got to Hickleton, where there is a long tight corner, the car landed up on the footpath at the wrong side of the road. That frightened me just as bad as any thing I had ever done before. I thought to myself 'I am going to get through the war without a scratch only to be killed on VE DAY' so I thought that discretion was the better part of valour and asked them to drop me off at Goldthorpe where I had some relatives. I had absolutely no intention of visiting my relatives there, but desperately needed to get as far away as possible from these very obliging two very drunk sailors. However one of my to regular 'lifts' came along and took home to Danby Dale.

At Denby Dale, exactly the same as plenty of other villages and towns, great celebrations were taking place. Tables were laid out in the middle of the road stretching from the Prospect Hotel to the White Hart. They were laden with all kinds of comestibles'; it was nothing short of miraculous where all the food came from. The village band played for dancing in the street. I remember someone playing an accordion.

Another playing a banjo a saxophone a violin. You can be sure we all enjoyed ourselves and supped the pubs out of beer and spirits.

However food rationing was to get worse rather than better, and it continued well into the fifties. Many food items were off ration by 1954 but meat rationing went on quite a bit longer. One thing always did puzzle, me it was when at times when there was a shortage of bread, we were told to eat potatoes, and they are good for you. Then surprise, at other times when there was a shortage of potatoes we were told to eat bread its good for you.

It reminds me of a quote from one of the Yankee Presidents "you can fool some of the people some of the time, and all the people some of the time. But you can't fool all the people all the time.".

Not long after I was taken ill and was admitted to the Station Sick Bay I felt really dreadful and pleurisy was diagnosed. I was taken to Doncaster Infirmary and I remember being left on a very draughty chilly corridor. I kept thinking my time had come. When I eventually got into a ward the care I received was first class, I recall sweating so much that I had to have the bed changed every few hours. The ward was full of other service men with various lung disorders; a few died while I was there. After a couple of weeks I was discharged and I went back to the station, and applied for some sick leave. The medical officer asked me' do you think you have been ill enough to qualify?" My reply was, "If I haven't I hope I never will be.

During that period we were living with my in laws at Leakhall Crescent , Denby Dale. We did get a house it was in the Nook, tucked away behind the Prospect Hotel. it was cold and damp , and very dreary, with large trees on three sides, We had no mod cons of any description almost like Victorian times. Luckily we did not have to stay there long before we got a two roomed flat at North View, in Denby Dale. This was a slight improvement but it left a lot to be desired. We went back to the same conditions that I had endured at Balls Row Kexborough, just one gas ring one gas light, and a coal fire with an oven and a side boiler. in order to have a bath we had to go to my in-laws, by the way I forgot to mention on of the amenities that we had at Kexborough, each house had a raintub, a wooden barrel that collected rain from the cottage roofs they held fifty gallons , and the water was kept for washing purpose. I have also not told you how we flitted from the nook to North View We used Joe Smith , he was a local 'gypsy type' chap , with a Gallower and flat cart. things were a bit different then there was no need for a proper removal firm as we did not have many belongings to move.

The people in the house above our living room were alright, we could not hear much from them except for their piano plating son. He was a good pianist but he practiced his scales a lot, which got on our wires a bit, but I suppose that is why he became so proficient. His dad also played the cornet in the local brass band, and he also practised a lot. We did not complain about that , we just got on with it . The room above our bedroom was fine in the daytime, but at night it was dreadful, they had two noisy children, nothing unusual about that. However they were allwed to stay up until god knows what time they would be playing ball games, or skipping or playing leapfrog. on top of all that most nights there was a grinding noise going on, what it was we never did get to know, but it was really infuriating. We were really fed up. So I confronted the chap and he said he could do what he liked in his own house, and threatened to knock my block off. My response was "alright if you want it that way I'll meet you in half an hour in the little wood" which was close by so he could have a go at me. He did not turn up but the noise abated after that we got on reasonable terms.

By December 1945 servicemen were beginning to be released, it was known as Class B release, and it was for essential workers, Mr Bishop got word to me that there was a shortage of railway signalmen. I knew that this job would be right up my street as l had been a signal box lad before the war. I applied and got demobbed just before Christmas. I was sent to Wembley Stadium football ground to hand in my uniform and equipment. We were supposed to hand in our Flying Log Book. but by chance the poweres that be never asked for mine. To say I was chuffed about this would be an understatement.It is now worth a bob or two I can tell you it would have to be a hell of a lot to make ma part with it. I have willed it to be handed to my first great grand son Adam Kelsall , when I have finally 'bought' it.

At Wembley I was issued with civies: a trilby hat , gabardine raincoat, shirt and tie (just the one)a grey chalk stripe suit(jacket and trousers

Top left, me showing off, Top right, just before an air test

Bottom left, sharpshooter, Bottom right, full crew 'Spirit of Russia' - this plane did over a hundred operations.

only) one pair of shoes, one pair of socks, I was allowed to keep my battle dress. Finally, the infamous Warrant Officer Sooty from my Blackpool days gave us a pep talk on how to cope with civilian life, remember that many had been in the forces for six years, some without getting home. I was very lucky to have been stationed close to home for the past twelve months. I was given fourteen days paid leave and had to go to Wakefield to be assesssed to see which kind of post I would be suitable for, with my experience I was went for training to be a signalman. My training was under taken at Lower Baraugh, near Barnsley I picked it up very quickly I already knew the majority of the bell signals and some of the procedure , For instance , if it was an ordinary passenger train we tapped three ,four for an express . there ere dozens of them . My biggest problem was Learning the rule book and the lock and block system, I will not even attempt to explain about that Because the signalman that was 'training' me turned out to be useless, I started to do a lot of studying at home. Then after about two weeks I found out that there was a vacancy at Darton which I applied for. I had to go to Wakefield again to be reassesed. It was a grade three Signalbox which meant that I would be jumping three grades up the 'pecking order' I would have been disappointed if I did not get the job, because I thought that I had done very well. I did get the job, the big snag about this was that because I was living at Denby Dale it meant an eight mile journey each way every day, I had managed to purchase a second hand bike to travel to work on, to enable me to wake up at the unearthly hour of four AM I had to acquire an alarm clock. To do so meant that I had to get a docket to buy one. as clocks were still on ration. Until I got one a kindly neighbour Mrs Whitwham lent me one. It did not bother me too much, having to cycle to work, except for when it was raining. Of course it was a different kettle of fish when it was snowing, sometimes I had to carry my bike. Eventually I bought a second hand motor bike, a 125cc Excelsior two stroke. It was fairly reliable but the front wheel coil spring broke and I could not get another one. I cobbled it together with some strong wire, very Heath Robinson-ish. I exchanged it for a 250cc BSA motorbike, ''Oh Calamity" I got it from a second hand dealer at Darton. on my first journey home, it seized up about a mile from home and I found it ever so embarrassing to have to push it for that final stretch. At the time I knew hardly any thing about motorbikes. Fortunately I had a friend

Wilf Mellor, who was a nap hand with them. I acted as his second-in-command while he repaired it for me, to do this we took the engine out of the frame and carried it into our basement flat, you see it was winter and I had no garage facilities. My wife was not too keen about this situation, but she just 'had to get on with it' we discovered that the side bearings had gone , one was completely shattered . actually it had worn away the casing. I managed to get some new ones in Huddersfield. however when we came to put new ones in. they sat very loose in the fittings. what we did then was pretty ingenious. We got a tin can , cut a strip off it we then wrapped this round the bearing and hammered it into the casing . Geronimo! it worked! But for how long? There was no way of knowing. Wilfs' advise was ''Flog it for what you can get'' Thus managing to recoup my outlay, and then I acquired a 500cc Rudge Special. Now we are talking, that was a decent bike. I had it for two or three years. and got a sidecar to put on it. The local Blacksmith had to make me some fittings to be able to attach it to the bike. it was a one seater, but with a bit of conniving I made it so that Bessie and my daughter could ride in it.

In1947I had made the bloomer of my life, by coming out of the RAF. I must have had a mental aberration(I had to look that one up in Rodget's Thesuraus)I must have been barmy! Being a Warrant Officer in the RAF meant that I had lots of privileges, plus fairly social hours. I was on about four pounds a week pay (It was probably more). Bessie's and Sandra's allowance would have been at least three pounds a week, plus free food and clothing for me that must have been worth at least one pound fifty a week. My Railway wage was, even with a grade three position was four pounds ten shillings a week gross, before union fees, Nation Insurance, etc. This meant that we were pretty stony broke for the majority of the time. But I stuck it out for a few more weeks. when the big snows of 1947started. the roads were so bad that I could not get to work some days. Something had to be done about this predicament, so I gave my notice in and got a different job at Kitsons Earthenware Pipeworks at Denby Dale, 'I was a wheeler in' which entailed wheeling the clay pipes to the coal-fired kilns to be fired, it was absolutely monotonous, but the wage was ten shilling a week more than the railway.

The Station Master at Denby Dale sent word to me that there was a position vacant at a signal box about three miles away. "The position is yours if you want it" I did not even consider it, as it was only a Grade One box, meaning a lower wage plus of coarse, some extra travelling would be involved. In contrast to Kitsons, that was ten minutes walk up the road.

Alas, conditions at the pipe works worsened. With the snow coming every day , it was difficult to get the clay to make the pipes, also the coal to fire the kilns with. Furthermore with road conditions being so atrocious, it was difficult to transport the product to where ever was necessary, on top of that , because of the big freeze , building sites where the pipes would be used , had come to a halt. Kitsons' did not lay anyone off but I could see the writing on the wall. also , by that time , with the snow and bad road conditions , coal which in any case was rationed, got very difficult for us to obtain coal to heat our damp basement flat. I think we were allowed one hundredweight a week, but some weeks we couldn't get any at all. I had to resort to begging coal from some collier friends. I fetched it in a kitbag from my RAF days, in Sandra's push chair. I should have been called a ' pullchair' because the snow was so deep that I had no chance of pushing it. I had to do this in the hours of darkness, because the colliers were not supposed to dispose of their coal by any means, whether it was sold or given away. But, because the flat was so damp and draughty , times were desperate. So I thought 'bugger this for a game of sodiers ' and I decided to go mining so that I could get some 'home coal'.

My mining career started at Parkmill Collliey, Clayton West. First of all I worked at the pit top, it was not a pleasant job, working outside in the extremely inclement weather, It was still snowing every day, like one of my rare sayings I 'Just had to get on with it'. After I had been there a few days I approached the manager to enquire about the possibility of having some 'home coal'. I explained about our damp conditions probably laying it on a bit heavy, you see I was supposed to work there for a month before I was allowed 'home coal. I said that I would be satisfied if I could fill a kit bag and take some home each day I would be very grateful he allowed me to have a ton delivered to my door two days later. we were then able to have a fire roaring up the chimney, it seemed very luxurious.

After two weeks or so I went to Lofthouse Colliery near Wakefield to train for underground work. By then the thaw had set in, and the rods were not too bad, so I was able to go on my motorcycle. The next problem was the scope of the ensuing floods. I came out of the mine one day and the road was two foot deep in water. I dare not drive through it so I had to push the bike through the water. It was very cold and very wet water, so you can imagine just how dreadful the twelve mile journey home was. The training was pretty basic, just the rudimentary elements of miming were drilled into us. Safety issues came to the forefront. The training lasted abut two weeks. Not long after this, there was a disaster at that mine, some uncharted workings were accidentally broken into, resulting in that face bring flooded and several miners were drowned. (the price of coal agian).

I then started at Springwood Colliery, on afternoon shift, I called it clock watching shift, this starting at two o'clock in the afternoon, to nine thirty at night. Before work you could do very little socially, likewise when you got home at night, after having a bath it was then bedtime. Pit head baths at Springwood arrived about seven tears later. Bathing at North View meant the tin bath in front of the fire. By that time we were able to buy a Burco gas boiler that eased the hot water situation, but because of the rationing still lingering on, we had to get another of the aforementioned 'dockets'. At that time wages were about seven to eight pounds a week.

My first job at Springwood was to be one of Harry Horn's' reykers'. Harry was well known for his 'utterances'. He used to say "wil't reyk me my pick / shovel / hammer" that meant, will you hand me my pick / shovel / hammer. Harry was over seventy years old and for his age he was remarkably nimble, and coped very well with the work. Our first job was heightening a 'gate' ie a roadway to make room for a Goliath Conveyer machine ie a belt conveying system Then I progressed to be trained for ripping', ie making road ways. After training I was joined by two other trainees and were put to work with two older men. however after a couple of weeks I found out that that the two older men were getting more wages than us. The pay structure was worked on what was called a 'butty system' a practice that had been outlawed in the industry several years previously I confronted the two men but got no response, so my friend Roy Hurst and I refused to work with them anymore, this resulted in us being kept at the pit bottom, near the 'shaft' for two days. it was very boring and very cold. the chap in charge ot the 'cage' (the lift for going up and down the shaft)was told that he must not. under any circumstances to let us up the shaft until the end of the shift. We went to the union rep about this, he did nothing, so we demanded to see the manager. And told him that we were being victimised. Human rights had not been heard of then he reluctantly had to agree with us. after that for several weeks, we were given the worst and lowest paid jobs available. I complained again to the over man that he was persecuting us and he sneeringly said "do you think you are good enough to rip a gate by yourself? "I said I am bloody sure I can" Eventually I did get the chance to prove myself and thus received a better wage.

After about two years I got a bit fed up with the afternoon shift so I went to Woolley Colliery as filler. That is on the face shovelling coal onto a conveyor belt. It was called a hand getting bord face, we had to shovel about fourteen tons onto the conveyor belt, plus of coarse, we had to support the roof with props. To help us on this job we had pneumatic picks neither cutting machines or blasting was allowed. it was a mucky dusty job but compared to ripping it was a lot easier. We alternated with day and afternoon shifts, so making things a bit more sociable. What with the stone dust and the coal dust , taking snuff and chewing tobacco and smoking cigarettes it is no wonder that my lungs are knackered. There were no such things as dust masks in those days, It was said that if you chewed tobacco it made you breath through your nose , thus filtering the dust. What a lot of bullshit.

On November 2nd1947 my second daughter Christine was born weighing in at a whopping ten pounds. She was like a three months old child, the first thing she did on this earth was to pee down Doctor Mitchells best suit He said "Ee Bessie I think this ones been here before" (Dr Dennis Mitchell was in his best suit because he 'd been to a local Christmas dance when the midwife got in touch with him. Christine made her grand entrance at nine o'clock in the evening, in her words "just in time for a light supper". I was on afternoon shift so I missed all the excitement. Next morning when the local midwife came along to bathe her , she was amazed to find that I had done all the necessaries, Christine was bathed, dressed, and all the rest. Plus I had prepared a steak and kidney pudding, and cleaned the flat. A neighbour Mrs Whitwham was a very big help to us at this time Yes, folks reckon this up, Christine's grand entrance came exactly nine months after the big freeze. Well we had to do something to keep warm. Shortly before Christine was born we had been able to obtain a a Silver Cross perambulator. it was and still is the Rolls Royce of prams. we were able to get it because we were friendly with the shop owner. (Clarence Bradbury at Skelmanthorpe)We actually walked home with it one Saturday evening with four year old Sandra sat up in it like the Queen of Shebba.

While Living at North View I used to help out at the nearby Cuckstool Farm(incidentally this is the place where the first famous Denby Dale Pie was made and cooked (more of that later) mostly I helped out with mucking out and the milk bottling. I was friendly with the owner Mr Heap who was farmer and butcher. I was paid with home cured bacon , milk and eggs. You see rationing was at that time at its worst. well I had to keep the wolf from the door, so what's the harm in a little skulduggery among freinds? Also where we lived we had an extremely unreliable gas supply, at night it would bob up and down like a brides nightdress. when milking was finished I used to borrow their Tilly lamp.

About that time I started keeping pigs , helped by a neighbour, Jack Marsden, between us we cobbled together a pigsty . that was difficult to do because of the scarcity of building materials. Jack was a driver for Naylor's who were earthenware pipe manufacturers. he obviously transported these pipes to building sites and somehow he managed to acquire some various bite and pieces, we also got a set pot , this was a cast iron vessel in the shape of a witches cauldron, we used this to boil up the swill to feed to the pigs,we had to get a permit to buy pig meal. Mrs Kendall a friendly shopkeeper, who shall be mentioned later, used to get us large bags of rough oatmeal.

Also from the farm I used to get the 'beastings' , these were the first milkings after the cows had calved. when the pigs got this ,their faces were wreathed in smiles, the second and possible third milkings were not suitable for the regular milk, so I used to take some home for Bessie to make Egg custard pies. These were absolutely delicious, yum yum, my mouth is watering at the thought of them. When the pigs were about eleven stones. We had them slaughtered by Skelmanthorpe Cooperative Butchers who had their own slaughterhouse. They salted the hams and bacon for us not because the task was beyond us, but for the simple reason that we hadn't the room to do it. Because we killed pigs we didn't get any bacon ration, but that was no hardship, we always had more than was sufficient for our needs. The offal was shared amongst relatives and friends. You see not many people had fridges and even fewer had deep freezers.

About this time I went down with a severe attack of influenza, several people have told me that they have 'worked on with he flu' do not believe them, but I was in bed for a week, four days of which I knew nothing about, I had to have my nightwear and bedding changed every few hours, because of the profuse sweating. I was off work for a month, and when I went back to work I was on light duties. recently I went to see my cousin Raymond, and he reminded me of this, apparently he came to see me when I was ill, and he thought I was a goner. It seems I juggled with Jesus and won once more. I know that for a long time afterwards I sweated a lot.

I stayed at Woolley colliery about two years, then I went back to Springwood Colliery and got a job boring holes in the coal for the shorfirers to blast the coal down, that was on the midshift, (eleven am to six thirty pm) it was a well paid, but the job was so repetitive that I was dreaming about it every night, so I asked to be taken off. I probably did the right thing , the amount of dust that borers were swallowing was awful . Borers were definitely high victims of Pneumoconiosis, ie Miners lung . another dreary period hit me then I became a market man. I was on a different job nearly every day , mostly the money was not god. so I moved again, in those days jobs were easily obtainable. I returned to Woolley Colliery as a developer- developing new faces. I was working with Harry Bedford (as mentioned earlier in my story)we had to develop a face with pneumatic picks it was not an easy job but we were paid a decent wage for it. Jimmy Talbot was our deputy what a character he was, very opinionated. What's more he had a first class degree with honours in telling porkie pies. But working with him meant that we were on a good rate of pay. But his stories! he once told us of a time when he had a motor cycle and side car. According to him , on one particular trip he lit a cigarette up on leaving Blackpool and was still smoking it when he reached Darton. Considering that this was a eighty mile journey , it must have been as long as his stories. You can imagine how may pinches of salt this tale was taken by us at that time. Also he told us that he had a fish and chip shop. According to Jimmy, one day his golden signet ring fell off into the boiling fat. He then automatically dipped his hand into the chip pan to retrieve it. Apparently he realised immediately that he had made a mistake(his words) but he said that he had the presence of mind to keep his hand in the boiling fat until someone brought a bucket of cold water for him to plunge his hand into. It was only slightly blistered when he took it out. Ho bloody Ho. However while he was telling these stories we were getting paid for doing nowt. At this time my wages were about twelve pounds a week. Somewhat improved when I worked at week ends, which I used to do if we wanted to purchase luxury items.

Christine was about one year old when we moved into a brand new council house at Clayton West. Whilst living at North View Denby Dale , I'm sure I wore a hole in the council office steps, I used to go there very often, complaining about the conditions we were living in. Also I badgered every councillor in the district, I suspect that they were so fed up with my protestations that they allowed me a new house simply to shut me up. It was situated at No 3 The Royds Clayton West approximately about six miles from Wakefield. It was a brand new property, a partly pre- fabricated building, it was a three bed-roomed house with all the mod cons and a toilet upstairs and down stairs (wow! what luxery) in addition there was an out house and a coal store, it was like moving into civilisation again. the flitting arrangements had now been upped a notch or two, this time we were going up in the world, we were flitted by a coal lorry, never broke a thing.

The back garden was part of a field that had been pasture for years, and also we had a fair sized front garden, which gave me plenty of scope to practice my gardening skills. I had a twelve by six foot greenhouse, which was heated by a coke fired boiler, also numerous cold frames. I raised a lot of bedding plants, vegetable and tomato plants, both for my own use and for sale. I tried to make a bob or two from my hobby to pay for the coke, I did not make any profit, but it gave me a lot of pleasure doing it. Year by year we acquired a lot of modern appliances, first of all was a electric vacuum cleaner, then a washing machine, this was a Hoover, it had not the slightest resemblance to the current versions, it had an impellor on the inside which did get the washing clean, but the clothes were really tangled up. The mangle was operated by the old fashioned britches arse steam it was attached to the top of the machine. And it was certainly better than the washing tub carbolic soap. rubbing board. posser and mangle of the 'good old days'.

Posser Poem.

When I was young a long time ago and not a posser high.
Mum used to take in the neighbours' wash for a bit o' brass to get by .
With her dolly tub, a rubbing board , carbolic ad dolly blue.
And a big old fashioned mangle, that was made of iron too
She'd heat the water with the fireplace boiler, so she could soften the carbolic soap.
What with the miner's muck, and the rubbing it took, it's a wonder she could cope.
The wringer was old and I was told, required some human power.
And me being her big lad, was volunteered for at least an hour.
She'd put the washing on't cloth hoist and raise it high.
O'er fireplace to drip on't flagstones until the washing was dry.
She'd iron all t'lot with an iron so hot, and put them in piles so neat
Each with their names on and numbers so i'd know where to tek them on't street.
When all was done she would say to me. come here lad i'm proud of thee"
S'ed give me a hug , ad a sloppy kiss, that's the part i'll allus miss .
I'm sorry to say , mam passed away , and lots of years have gone by.
But'I'll make a bet she does the washing yet. Up in that sky.

Then we got an electric powered radio instead of the old battery set. following on we purchased an electric cooker. , refrigerator and a twelve inch bush television. We got this just previous to the opening of the Holme Moss Transmitter. Prior to that the signal came from Sutton

Coldfield, but we only received a poor picture from there. the first programme that we got from Holme Moss was of Terry Thomas and Peter Butterworth, who were supposedly stood on top of the mast, it would have been mighty cold if it had been true. Television prices have not escalated with inflation a twelve inch Bush cost £64.(black and white only in those days) You can get a fourteen inch colour television for less than that now. (I am surprising myself with my memory) I wish my typing and spelling was as good.! Before long we had amassed an array of modern electric appliances, an iron, a toaster and a vacuum cleaner, Our previous vacuum cleaner was fly-wheel operated by Britches arse steam,(I believe all these 'mod cons' are on the wedding list now)

Shortly after getting the television, financial circumstances dictated that I got a better job. I went on the afternoon shift. this meant that I could only watch television at week ends, you see programmes finished at ten thirty PM, there was no day time viewing what so ever they finished at ten thirty at night. I came home from work to find three neighbours watching our television. Plus there was no supper ready for me. Bessie went across to the fish and chip shop for my supper, to say I was cross was a bit of an understatement. When she got back with the fish and chips and put them on a plate for me , I got hold of the plate and threw the lot on the fire and said to the ladies "now you lot can bugger off so that Bessie will have time to get me some proper supper ready" I said if you think I am slogging my guts out to pay for other peoples entertainment you must think I have come in on the Banana boat. it did not happen again. The high light of the early television days was, of coarse , the Coronation of Queen Elizbeth 11 I did invite some neighbours to come in to watch that.

When I was a child and lived with my grandma ad granddad, nearly all their children had to learn to play the piano. My sister did too. When it came to my turn I think that they had got fed up listening to a lot of scales and playing a lot of unmelodious tunes so they never asked me if I wanted to learn. I was quite pleased about that ,it meant that I could go out lakin with me mates. I have regretted it ever since, so when my children were old enough I bought them a second hand piano, which did not last very long because it came from a very damp house. When it came to our very warm house ie the board on which the wires are strung, dried out. consequently it soon went badly out of tune. So I asked some one to retune it, he informed me that this was not possible because it had dried out too much. that I am afraid it meant a lot more aching bones to pay for a new one. We went to a shop in Eldon Street in Barnsley to look at some. We got the best we could not afford. If my memory serves me right it cost two hundred and fifty pounds it was on the never never of coarse. They took the dried out one in part exchange. I do not what we got for it Whoops!! I forgot to mention the dried out board. I heard one of the neighbours saying "where do they get the money from.". over hearing this I said to them "We get the money from the same source as you do, from working but we don't swill it down our throats at the pubs and clubs as you do" At that time , also at many different periods in my life since I have been able to stop smoking so that I could pay for little extras, unfortunately the Parkinson piano playing did not last very long Sandra and Christine had both started to get the hang of it, when we moved to Denby Dale Bessie would not let them travel back to their teacher at Clayton West for lessons. Also she would not agree to let them having a new tutor in Denby Dale, because she had changed music lessons when she was a child and she ha not liked it, as each teacher had their own style and it got confusing, I have wished since that I had put my foot down and gone against her wishes.

I had done seven years at the coal face when I decided that I had not been put on this earth to use a pick and shovel so I enrolled at Barnsley Mining and Technical College to study for Deputy and Shotfirers Certificates. I had to attend the 'Tech' as it was called, in the mornings when I was on the afternoons and in the evenings when I was on day shift. I also had to study for a Certificate in First Aid I found it a bit hard going . But I did have 'Percy ' on my side 'good old Mr Verance'. The oral exams were taken at the 'Tech' the practical exam was at the Springwood Colliery Clayton West The Manager there was the Examiner, several safety features had been deliberately planted. When we finished the manager told me that I had done very well and he offered me a job as a shot firer, I asked him what shift I would be on. He said on night shift for a start and after a few weeks I would be able to go on dayshift, which for shot firers was from five am to twelve thirty in the afternoon. these hours had not troubled me when I worked at Woolley Colliey which was seven miles from Clayton West it meant that I had to get up at four thirty just the same. I decided that I would take the job at Springwood Colliery. At Woolley Colliery my Under Manager Bert Schofield sent for me whist I was working my notice, he asked me if I would stay on if he offered me a shot firers position. he promised me that I would not to do that for very long before he gave me a deputies job. I was tempted but I had to consider the traveling time and the different shits that I would have to work their it was a non starter. However I must say that I was much happier at Woolley Colliery Than I ever was at Springwood Coliery, I always thought that Bert appreciated my endeavours more.

The seams at Springwood were, Wheatley Lime, which was not a first class coal ,it was two foot six thick inches thick, the other seam was New Hards. That was eighteen inches thick when the rock was cut from underneath it , that made it three more inches, this was very good coal ,I never had to do any filling on that face, but I did a lot of shot firing. this job was a doddle. According to Coal mines regulations shot firers are not allowed to fire more than eight shots per hour. We went on two hours before the fillers ad we had to fire our forty shots off before they arrived or we could not fire them because the conveyor belt would be running . we had to lay on the belt to fire our shots. If the Coal Mines Act 1911 had been strictly adhered to, coal would have been a lot dearer.

I did most of the jobs as an official at Springwood. Walking the boundary was one that I quite enjoyed. that was examining the roadways that did not come under deputies districts. A lot of legging came into it, however there were ways and means of avoiding the legging, but I will not go into that. The best part of it was that at different parts of the mine I came to the surface and was able to cadge a cup of tea and a fag.

The worst job was firing for a new drift. On this job we were allowed to fire six shots at a time. After each shots I had to walk back through the dust and fumes. and fire the next round. It probably contributed to the lung problems that I have now. At one point I was the union delegate. I took this job on reluctantly. I had opened my big gob at at union meeting about the previous delegate, he promptly resigned and I was proposed for the job and I could not very well refuse. I was picked out of the hat at a delegates meeting in Barnsley to go to a labour party summer school in Dorking Fortunately I had informed the under manager about this, but my lackadaisical union secretary should have informed the manager in writing he had not done so. The day before I was going the manager told me that he had not been informed about it , and told me that I could not go. You see the manager and I. Had a reciprocal agreement, we hated each others guts, of course I did go, I had arranged to take another delegate in my car and I could not let him know what had happened. Whist I was away the manager sent a hand-delivered letter to my wife stating that he was terminating my employment at Springwood Colliery. By the way the Under Manager was on holiday at the time so I could not ask him to confirm that I had informed him. When I got back the manager would not allow me to give him any explanation whatever. The local president and Secretary did very little to get me reinstated so I went over there heads to see Larry Wormald the national secretary of my Union, whose headquarters are at Barnsley. Whilst I was in his office he rang up my manager and told him in no uncertain terms that he had handled the situation in a most undemocratic manner, and he must reinstate me immediately and inferred that if not, the officials at his mine may down tools. Next day the manager called me in to his office and said that due to the circumstances he had been wring to sack me . I would like to have told him about his conversation with Mr Wormald but for once I controlled my tongue. I was not the only one who did not like the manager almost every one hated his guts. When I came out of the office that day , the office staff silently applauded me. That was nice! my wages at that time were seventeen pounds a week and two pounds extra when I was a Deputy.

David Pell was a friend of my childhood. And after the war we renewed our friendship. This only lasted a few years as both he and his wife were always broke and were forever on the cadge, one evening after we had been visiting their home, he volunteered to take us home in his newly acquired second hand car. When we got nearly back to our village he noticed that he was almost out of petrol. Very few filling stations opened on a Sunday evening then, Luckily I was friendly with a local publican who also owned a nearby filling station. We called at his pub and asked if he would open up for us. that he grudgingly did, his garage was a fair distance from the pub. My 'friend' asked him to put half a gallon in the tank, I will never forget the look on the publicans face. I said ''Fill it up and I will pay for it", Uncle Hector told me not to lend them any money he knew that I would not get it back, so we quietly dropped them. One of his expressions I will never forget was "he was as clumsy as a toad with a muck fork" - when he was referring to anyone who was inept.

As in all villages , local characters were in abundance, at Clayton West we had our fair share. On was Billy Mixup-no kidding I never knew his real name, he was rather 'work shy'. When seeking work he always asked a negative question, such as "You are not setting anyone on today are you" another character had the curious name of Albert Wardrobe Robinson, his father had the same name, The mind boggles (Jumping off the wardrobe to conceive springs to mind) when asked the state of his health, he was the one who coined one of my sayings, "I am a little bit better than I was before I was as bad as what I have been"! The drummer in the local Brass Band was about five foot tall , it was said that on one occasion the band were walking and playing around the village at Christmas. At a fork in the road the band went one way and he went another,(True?).He worked down the mine, and for his size he was a good worker. He once told me that he had not started growing until he was seventeen , but then he had shot up like a willow. A lot of the villagers had nick names one of them was 'Symphonic Flush' he was the local plumber. There were many more but sorry to say I can not remember them. Kexborough folk were called Keckers or Kespers . Skelmanthorpers were called Shatters, another name for them was 'Shat earhole biters' this was because some one had an ear bitten of in a fight. We don't seem to get these colourful characters nowadays do we? All people north of Kexborough were called 'Yarsiders' (Yarside is Yorkshire Dialect for was for an outsider.) Herman Shaw was a local farmer, who often said "there is always some kind of weather at this time of the year". He delivered his milk by the traditional method of horse drawn milk float, no resemblance whatsoever to the modern milk float, his last call of the day was at the Shoulder of Mutton public house in Clayton West. He stayed there until he was nicely lubricated just as well that the horse knew its way home! It was said that he fastened his horse to the shafts with binder twine because he would never be able to unharness it in his state of inebriority. When I worked at Woolley Colliery one chap would constantly ask me "what's it like isn't Yarside Foothills this morning". You see I lived about seven miles away in the Yarside hills.

Another laughable thing happened while I was working at Springwood, During the pit holiday week a chap called Albert Dyson a night shift 'Daytler' (as non face workers were called) went to Blackpool for the week. Albert was a middle aged man who lived with his mother, one day he got so drunk in the afternoon, that he fell asleep in one of the tram shelters on the Promenade. On that day there was a day trip from his village to Blackpool. And some of the lads came across Albert in his drunken stupor in the shelter, and took it upon themselves to 'deliver him safely home 'to his mother'...we've brought your Albert home, we found him on the prom ''He will not be best pleased about that he had gone there for the week'', She said. I wonder what his land lady at Blackpool thought of it when he did'nt get in for the 'lights out'.

At Springwood there was a ripper called Eric Mitchell, he was a big strong lad who was going to 'Tech' to study for his Managers ticket He was a tailgate ripper and his gate was a credit to him, he ripped the gate on his own. However, on his day at the 'tech it took two men to do the same as he did single handed, I remember when he had finished his shift one day and he came across two pipe fitters who were struggling with a large four way cast iron junction besides a tub, out of the goodness of his heart he picked it up and plonked it in the tub for them. "Nay Eric , we've nobbert just struggled to get it out of theer" they muttered. Mind you they were only dwarfs compared to him. Eric Went on to be a general manager of Yorkshire District Mines If my memory serves me correctly the afore mentioned Basil Clegg trained him to be a wrestler. Another of his feats was a drift that he and his father developed,

what its purpose was I can not remember, but I have never seen anything as neat down a mine , it looked like it had been carved by a machine it was a one in four gradient and was supported by ring girders , and slabbed by concrete slabs and stepped all the way down. I met his wife a year ago , and she said that she had a photograph of it I wish I had one

In those days the holes that were bored in both coal and stone were drilled by pneumatic hand held drills that shook the bones out of your body. They were noisy and heavy and very dusty. The six foot long drills had to be carried out each dy to be sharpened by he blacksmith. Later these were replaced by tungsten knock on and knock off bits. These were obviously a lot lighter to carry. Later still his coal borers got lighter compressed air drills and much lighter tungsten bits, these were easier to use but caused a lot more dust.

At Springwood tools were provided free of charge, at Woolley we had to pay for them. We got free shovels when they were worn out. Regular face workers had to lock their ' tackle' up or you could not find them next day. Market men (that is men who do not have a regular job) had to carry there tools from the pit bottom to the face. They were paid one and sixpence a day for it. At Springwood rippers had to pay for their explosives fillers got it free. At Woolley it was free for all.

If the I R A had been at their shenanigans in the fifties they would surely had a field day at the explosives magazine at Springwood. It just had a wooden door, it was well away from the other buildings and just secured by a flimsy padlock. Both the explosives and the detonators were stored there. The containers that the explosive was carried down the mine in. Were very flimsy Fred Carno type contractions. They were made out of old belting and fastened by a staple and a bit of wire. When a new manager arrived at Springwood and saw them, he immediately got some proper ones made of metal which could only be opened by a shot firers key. There were various types of explosives, two types for coal some for dry conditions and some for wet. These two contained their own flash inhibitor. Another was Ajax (which won a noble peace prize) which was contained in a paper sheath that was for using on stone, which also contained a flash inhibitor. I 'think' it was baking powder.

At Woolley we had to pay for the chalk to mark the motty numbers, on the tubs (each face had a different number). At Springwood the fillers were able to choose the length of their stint according to their ability. The stints varied from fourteen to eighteen yards approximately a ton and a Quarter to the yard. At Woolley it varied according to the thickness of the coal seam. In the Siltstone Seam where I worked it was twelve yards, not an inch more! We more or less relied on getting a lot of waiting time, because we were always waiting for tubs. That in my mind was very bad management. Also at Woolley, we were paid on one note for the face, and got shares according to the number of shifts that you had worked we had a charge hand, who every week had to go begging to the under manager for extras. - Usually we got perhaps one to two shillings a day. Then it was up to the charge hands honesty how it was shared out! I often had my suspicions? Another stupid thing that used to happen on afternoon shift, some of Fridays coal did not get out of the pit until Monday morning , so the charge hand had to get that separately . That's the way it was, bloody crackers! Each tub was weighed at the pit head I suspect that a lot were booked down to average weight two men were employed to do this, one for the owners and one for the workmen. These were called check weight men, if I remember rightly one was called Elijah Benn. He was a top union man it was more than rumoured that he and other union officials were corrupt, but nothing was ever proved. A chap called Jim Conway worked on our face; I think he was a union delegate. He was a very good negotiator. Alas he wasn't very muscular, he had to be helped out with his stint occasionally, I suspect thane had communist leanings. Alas later he committed suicide. The hand getting faces that I worked on in the Siltstone Seam were long wall faces about a hundred yards long two tail gates and a main gate. Our stints were usually nine yards long, but they varied according to how many turned up for work, if we had to do extra yards we did not advance so far. Normally we would advance about five to six foot a day. When I first started at Woolley, the under manager asked me if I had ever used a 'windy pick', that is a Pneumatic pick I said yes of cause (I had seen one before). So he started me on a filling job, I had a stint of my own. After a fortnight my records came through from Springwood, the safety officer noticed that had not been trained as a filler, so I was told to go and see the under manager , he said that he had good reports from my deputy , otherwise he would have sacked me. Instead I had to go training with filler for six weeks. On the first face I worked on we had to use the windy picks quite a lot because if the conditions. The second face was quite different, the roof was controlled by building packs in the gabbing waste with the used wooden props, and the roof never broke. This very even pressure on the coal face made it easier to get. In fact, before long I hid my steel for the windy pick under a sleeper and never used it again.

At Springwood , we all had cap lamps, but at Woolley when I first went there not all had cap lamps , I had to carry what was called a bucket lamp I have been told that they weighed about eight pounds. Well when walking downhill to the workings the air was not too bad, because it was facing you , but when you were walking out and the air was behind you, and being knackered, the lamps seemed to weigh two stones if you had to carry tools as well, it was bloody hard work. And there are no cups of tea down the mine.

On the development face where I worked with Harry Beckford, we only use windy picks an britches arse steam. We had to head out a face on the bord, about eight wide, this was to develop an end face, it was very hard work, and we only had cloth tube bagging for ventilation. we had extend the bagging and the conveyer as we went along, Occasionally we persuaded our deputy to fire us some flanking shots, which were strictly illegal. We had to shovel the coal onto the belt, which just dropped off the conveyer onto the floor in the gate. then four or five times a shift we had to ride down the belt and fill it into the tubs .There were still some wooden tubs in the pit. They did not hold as much coal as the mettle ones, so we got the gate end lads to sort some wooden ones out for us each day. We seemed to get better weight on our pay tickets. As I said before the weigh men obviously gave a lot of average weighs on a lot of tubs. We had a Pony to bring in the empties and take away our full ones. Pit Ponies are very intelligent. They could definitely count. If you put an extra tub on, they could count the links and would not move. We also had to watch out our 'snap', or they would eat it paper and all. We used to take them tit bits; they would also eat your apple or orange while it was still in your pocket. We were not allowed to ride on them, and I never did because I never got the chance. But it did help when you were waking out of the pit if you could hang on to their harness or tail. A far as I know, they were very well treated at Woolley Colliery. By the way if the ponies did not get you 'snap'. The mice would have it. At Springwood the problem was rats. Paper wrappings were banned and we had to get 'snap' tins. Also water bottles were banned as so many miners were getting cut with broken glass.

While I was a delegate at Springwood, I want to a Labour Party Summer School in Dorking, it had been donated to the labour Party by Sidney and Beatrice Webb who were staunch Labour Party supporters. There I got 'second' hand knowledge about the bed swapping that goes on at these places, I could enlarge, I would probably be sued for libel. I was also chosen to go to the Labour Party Annual Summer conference at

Blackpool. The shenanigans were the order of the day, it is said that the Conservative party have similar leanings. Must be something to do with the sea air.

While I was secretary of my local union branch, I discovered that we had no pepper written agreement for our home coal allowance. I brought this up at the next meeting, and suggested that we should try to get the same agreement as the officials at Woolley Colliery they got a lot better quality of coal than the ordinary workers had. They had to pay abet extra for this. How ever I was voted down and we got the same agreement as the workmen. Whilst in that position I also introduced as scheme where we had to contribute a shilling a week to fund the Christmas present for retired officials, Plus to floral tributes to deceased members just one person opted out of that scheme that was Walter Skelton the afternoon over man. he Ranted on at me about the scheme in front of the workmen so much, I immediately went out of the pit and saw the manager about it, the manager made him apologise to me in front of the men.

When I started to work down the mine a lot of the miners still wore clogs. So did I. I had a good little sideline going when I worked at Woolley. There was a clog maker in the village where I lived, he made very good clogs and charged me ten bob a pair for them. I sold them on for twelve and sixpence. Inferior clogs cost fifteen shillings on Barnsley Market. tHe clog maker was quite a character he used to say '' Does' than work in water'?' if you said yes he would charge sixpence extra. I could not see any difference in them. Then he would ask, ''does than want slurring irons on'' if so it was another sixpence. Not many will know what slurring irons are, in those days miners had irons on their clogs, both sole and heel. Slurring irons were small ones that fitted in the sole. They just fitted over the narrow pit railway rails, so the trimmers could slide along the rails when it was down hill journeys. Not many wanted them; they would have been popular in the times before conveyer belts. Later clogs were frowned upon and employers advised us to wear safety boots. The first pair I got, my dog took a fancy to them, and ate the lace holes out of one boot. I had to fasten it with a thin lather belt or I could not have nor to work.

I was the afternoon Shift deputy for a development area, it was a new heading. The day shift cut and filled the coal, and the afternoon shift ripped the roadway. It was a six foot by twelve foot ripping. Two 'men' did it. They were the most avaricious 'men' that I have had the misfortune to come across. They had reported my predecessor and got him sacked. Apparently he had a miss fire that is when a detonator has not gone off. Albert Littlewoods was his name, it broke the poor fell. When you have a miss fire you were obliged to take it to the safety officer, who sent it to a Mines Research place near Buxton to be tested. .Well Albert like many others including myself plunged this detonator into a big wad of stemming clay and fired it. Very often the detonator was not faulty, it was usually the cable. I appealed to the manager to save his job, but to no avail. The manager told me he had no option. It was a stackable offence he had to sack him. Albert was about sixty at the time, he was never the same man again. When I had fired the shots for these 'men', they had to fetch a girder from about twenty yards back down the gate. They asked me how much I was going to pay them to fetch it. I said two shillings, and they laughed and said that they wanted ten shillings. They sent for the over man to arbitrate. When he arrived he said "What's the problem?" and he said that he would give them an extra sixpence. Then he said, "all the time I have been coming to you, I have been wondering which of you was buried and how much the other wanted paying to dig him out"? When that job was finished the over man gave them the worst jobs he could find. That pleased me and my compatriots down to the ground. By the way I did manage to save Albert's pension rights.

The first holiday after the war was to Fleetwood. This was when Bessie was pregnant with Christine, and instead of going by coach as usual, we went by private hire taxi, in consideration of Bessie's 'delicate' condition. My Dad and Stepmother went with us, and the weather was absolutely glorious. The weather was perfect for the entire week that we spent there. I remember it well, because it was at the time when miners at one pit in South Yorkshire (I think it was Grime Thorpe) were on strike because of one extra foot of coal that the management wanted to put on to their stints. They were on strike for about ten weeks.

At that time the annual entitlement for holidays was one week paid, plus Bank holidays. The mines closed down completely for that week, except for safety workers, for obvious reasons. There was just one year during that era when we stayed at home for the annual holiday. We decided that we could not afford to go that year. In reality it seemed to cost more going out on day trips and outings than it would have cost going for the week. Almost every year that we lived at Clayton West we had a week's holiday at Blackpool. We used to stay with Miss Riley, at 22 Crystal Road. I think the charges for an adult were Seventeen shillings and sixpence a day full board. When we first started going there, rationing was still on, but Miss Riley seemed to feed us pretty well. I remember sitting at our table one week and watching the antics of a couple at another table, whose names escape me, but I think that they lived at Shipley. At every meal time they drank all the milk and emptied the sugar basin into a paper bag to take home with them. They left nothing edible on the table. When they'd finished every meal, the cruet must have felt very lonely on the tablecloth on the last day I could not contain myself any longer. I said to them you have for gotten something. You have not emptied the salt and pepper. They did not even blush.

While in Blackpool we always went to three or four shows, there was an abundance to choose from. I remember once when sitting on the Central Pier we got chatting to Albert Medley, a very popular comedian of that time. At Feldman's Theatre we saw Joseph Locke the Irish tenor, Ruby Murray, Bob Monkhouse and many others. At the Grand Theatre there was George Formby, Freddie Brinton and Thorax Hard. Reggie Dixon was resident organist at the Tower Ballroom with his mighty Wurlitzer. Bernard Brandon and his wife Barbara Kelly appeared at the Hippodrome (later to become the ABC cinema) it was there that we first heard Ken Dodd's rendition of 'On the road to Mandalay'. Tommy Tinder appeared regularly at the North Pier. We watched may a good play at the Repertory Theatre in Tinsley Street near to the Manchester Hotel. They changed their programme twice a week so that holiday makers could see two different plays during their week's stay, this was a practice that cinemas used up and down the country. We and others thought that Blackpool was the tops it is a different kettle of fish now.

Around this time 'we' (mostly me I'd kike to point out) decided to better our housing position by buying our own property. We made enquiries about several properties, but one by one, for different reasons them ere eliminated. Then one at Danby Dale came up which we liked. It was a three bed roomed Bungalow. In a very nice position. With a generous garden and a large conservatory, it was centrally heated and was said at the time. to be considered to be a gentleman's residence. We paid one thousand seven hundred and fifty pounds for it, when the average price for bungalows was one thousand two hundred and fifty pounds. We could not afford it. But we still bought it. All my friends and relations told me I was wrong in the head even contemplating it. However I just got on with it yet again… I consider it was the best thing I ever did. It got me some collateral. The Co-operative Insurance Society provided the mortgage for Twelve hundred and fifty pounds; the remainder was raised by selling a couple of insurance policies and a private loan. This was without a written agreement from my friend Mrs Kendall, who owned a shop in Danby Dale. This I paid of as soon as I could, by working Saturdays and Sundays at a local electrical shop repairing kettles and irons and other bits and pieces. Plus I helped out at a local fish and chop shop rumbling potatoes.

We had now 'arrived' in the house removing stakes (Known in Yorkshire as flitting) and employed Pickfords a 'proper' removal firm. With the appropriate vehicle this time. The bungalow was called The Gables; superficially it was a little run down. However over the years we licked it into the shape that suited us. Central heating was not as widespread as nowadays at The Gables it was powered by a coke fired boiler. I soon discovered that it could be fired by coal. It fairly gulped down the coal. But 'home coal' was very cheap, and one or two you my workmates let me have some of their allocation. This was a bit dicey, because as I have told you before 'Home coal' was meant solely for the personal use of the miner. Who said life was straightforward? I had three accidents down the mine whilst living in the bungalow. First I crushed a couple of ribs. The next one was a bit more severe. I badly injured my back and landed up in Pinderfields Hospital at Wakefield, I had to sleep on a board for a long time. The Consultant at Pinderrfields was a Miss Pearson and when she discharged me said. You have a cracked bone in your spine. And that I was going to have a lot of pain for a long time. How right she was!

Whilst at The Gables I acquired my first motor car. It was a Morris 10 saloon. There I taught myself to drive. I was very naughty and did not always have a qualified driver accompanying me for every journey, but I never drove without the L plates until I passed my test. One afternoon, when my wife had gone to the chapel, Christine and I went for a short ride to the next village. Taking our dog Ladie with us. At one point while negotiating a tight corner. Another dog came bounding out at us. Ladie took exception to this and went quite berserk in the back of the car. He landed up on my shoulders, causing me to run into a flimsy dry stone wall. At the local cricket field. Immediately I contacted the secretary at the club and told that I would rebuild the wall. There were no repercussions from this luckily I only broke a lamp glass on the car. As son as I arrived home I put the car in the garage so that Bessie would not see it before I managed to replace the glass. Christine was sworn to secrecy. However we have both had a little chuckle about it since. It was a lovely car even though it was about twenty years old. There were only a few thousand miles on the clock when I got it, the reason being that a gent's outfitter at Clayton West was the previous owner. And it was said that the car had never been out of the district, the engine was in very good condition , but it had a broken chassis that had been bolted together by two mining fish plates it was very well done. We had some very good outings in it, and it never failed us. At that time the Mot was just about to appear on the scene, and I thought that this car would not pass the stringent test. So I exchanged it for a second hand AustinA40. Which I paid £300 pounds for. I kept this for twelve months, in that time I had spent another £300 on it in repairs. I decided there and then that I would never buy a second car again. I traded that in for a brand new blue Ford Anglia van; this was to prove extremely useful before long.

Whilst living in the bungalow I broke several ribs in another mining accident. After !8 years working underground, this put me my thinking cap on, It caused me to decide that that mining was not destined to be my future. A very lucky thing happened. Whilst recuperating from these fractured ribs I learned that a local greengrocers business in Danby Dale was for sale. The business was owned by Eva Kendall's son Richard. I delved further into the financial side of the venture and decided to have a go at it, Father-in law (Basil) tried to dissuade me. He

Top, first Paddy train at Woolley Colliery

Bottom, New lockers just before the mine was closed.

said that it was beyond my capabilities and too risky. (Such confidence fair bucked me up) I got an appointment with Richard Kendall's bank manager in Leeds for a loan. This was in 1963 he questioned me on my abilities to see if I had any idea about bookkeeping, maths and other relative things, I outlined my previous jobs and experience, and got I a loan without any trouble. I had to admit that I had no selling experience. I said that I thought that I was a quick learner. Fortunately I had been union secretary of my local branch for the past two years. Each year I had to produce a balance sheet, sodas at least slightly familiar with figures. I had absolutely no problems with selling my bungalow. My friend Eva Kendall was ready to retire and purchase it at the same price that I had paid for it. Property inflation had not yet reared its ugly head, and in my position I was in no position to bargain because I wanted a quick sale. Any way with the bank loan and the proceeds from the sale of the bungalow I managed to scrape enough money together to go into the business. The house, which was leasehold, plus the shop and the mobile shop, cost about three thousand five hundred pounds. Incidentally, my solicitor was not in favour of me buying the business, he said I was stretching myself too far. However with out question, I can say I have been stretching myself all my life, and quite categorically that buying the bungalow was the best move liver made in my life. It was a 'stepping stone' to a better (life) WORK???

As I was financially stretched when I purchased her son's business, Eva Kendall came to the rescue once more. She gave me another loan to purchase the stock. Again no agreement was signed. We trusted each other implicitly. I still have the little red book with each repayment recorded in it. Frank Kendall (Eva's husband) was quite a character; he was Chief Clerk at a local mill. With a very drill since of humour. Frank was a dab hand at figures. and could tot up three columns simultaneously . Eva was a very accomplished cook and Frank used to say that when the relatives descended on them for a meal he used to urge her to make them a Seasoned Yorkshire Pudding with plenty of oatmeal in it. This was so that it would expand in their belier and so fill them up before they got to the meat course, in those days it was served as an appetiser; however in Frank's eyes he wanted it act in the opposite way. Another of his stories was going into The Crown Hotel at Cosset. There was no one else in the pub or the bar. Frank said that he let off a 'stocking footer' IE a silent but deadly fart. whEn the barmaid came in and caught a whiff of this she lifted one foot and then the other as if she had trod in some dog shit ''So I did the same '' said Frank.

We moved into the shop a month later. Again we used Pickford as removal van even we were just going down the road. With a business being involved we simply hadn't the time to mess about. Moving bits and bats at a time. We needed a 'professional job doing. It was indeed a good business. Bloody hard work and very long hours. Sixteen hour days were not unusual, that was of the mobile shop, which was a purpose built Comer Diesel complete with all the necessary fitments. Apart from selling greengrocery I sold fish, flowers and plants. With a wide range of groceries and cakes. I also had a separate confectionary and chocolate cabinet. How I kept the fish fresh in summer, I don't know, but I never had a complaint. I used to fill it up as much as I could with ice from the fish market. But that didn't last very long on hot days I kept it in a special box under the counter with a lid on it. There was a hole in the corner to let the water out. It must have left a bit of a pong at the place where I stood for a long time. However that did not happen very often I had to move from house to house, because no way did Mrs Smith want Mrs Jones to know her business. You got to know quite a bit about peoples' financial status, especially on new estates. One customer even asked me if she could have a half pound of peas, kidney beans. And broad beans. How the hell I Kept my face straight I don't know. At the end of the month, on these estates they always had a let of coins; they were scraping up their loose coins, or emptying their piggy banks to buy essential foodstuffs.

Danby Dale is famous for its enormous meat and potato pies. The first one was made in1788 to commemorate the 'recovery' to health of King George111 he was the one that lost his marbles. Not much is known about this pie. The second one was in1815 to celebrate Wellington's victory over Napoleon Bonaparte at the Battle of Waterloo. The third one was in1846 that was to celebrate the repeal of those terrible Corn Laws, which caused riots up and down the country. People starved to death because of the price of flour. In those days bread was the staple diet of the country. In 1887 the fourth pie was to celebrate the Golden Jubilee of Queen Victoria's reign. This was a disaster, professional chefs were employed to make this pie, and the recipe included several types of game plus various dubious meats, consequently, when the pie was opened the stench was overpowering. The chef departed the village at speed. It was decided to give it a good Christian burial in quick lime in Toby Wood. Memorial cards were printed as follows.

Strong was the smell that compelled us to part
From a treat to the stomach and a salve to the heart
Like the last Danby Dale pie which the crowd did assail
Its contents a rank mixture, it quickly went stale
Though we could not eat it yet we still lingered near
'till the stench proved too much for our nasals to bear.
So, like sensible men, the committee did say
'Taws better to inter it without further delay

A card was distributed to Denby Dale villagers the following week and a note at the bottom said.

Undeterred by previous efforts the people of Denby Dale have attempted another pie, which is to be consumed today (Saturday)and it is expected to be a success .Forty eight stones of flour, ninety six stone of potatoes ,two stone of onions, a heifer, and two sheep were the ingredients.

During WW11 the pie dish was dug up broken and auctioned off. The proceeds of the sale went towards the building of a Spitfire. The fifth pie was to celebrate the fiftieth anniversary of the Repeal of the terrible Corn Laws. You would think that the next one would be just after the WW1, but due to the state of the availability of food, and the awful consequences on the economy this was delayed until 1928.This pie was to raise £1.000 for Huddersfield Infirmary. The first commemorative plate was made for Queen Victoria; in fact two plates were issued at the lime. These plates are now very much collectors items, and will be worth upwards of three hundred pounds. I have no idea how much they cost when new. I have a slight recollection of the 1928 pie. My grandma went to the celebrations and purchased a commemorative plate for two shillings and sixpence.

In 1963 the idea of another pie was muted by a few friends who mulled it over for a while, and then decided to have a meeting at the Memorial

Hall to see if it could raise enough interest in it. The meeting proved fruitful and it was decided to go ahead, so the next pie was in September 1964. The proceeds were used to purchase a large house in Danby Dale to be converted into a meeting place, and it became known as The Pie Hall. It wasn't decided what the pie was going to commemorate. Luckily four Royal births occurred in 1964, so this became the excuse. Outside the t Pie Hall stands the Pie Dish, which is now used as a flower bed. Its dimensions are, eighteen feet long, six foot wide, and eighteen inches deep. Some pie!! A plate was commissioned to commemorate the occasion. The price was seven and six pence. I sold quite a lot in both my shop and my mobile shop. Other memorabilia included mugs. One person in the village has a full dinner service, inclusive of tureens, depicting the 1928 pie, this must now be priceless. The 1964 pie was made and baked in a newly built cowshed, belonging to Hector Buckley at Dry Hill Farm, Dunkirk. To enable them to do this, the meat, potatoes and onions were cooked in BARCO Boilers. All the local butchers were involved in cutting the beef up. Which was locally reared? Dozens of people were involved in the peeling and cutting up the potatoes all the local bakers each made large portions of crust. When the meat and the potatoes were fully cooked they were tipped into the pie dish, which had baffle plates inside to stop the gravy being sloshed out. The reason for this was that the pie was transported on a trailer around the village to the field where the pie was to be served. During the journey a few steep inclines bad to be negotiated. It was towed by a Steam Traction Engine which had a generator on it to keep the pie at the proper temperature, whilst it was being transported. Heaters were put in each section of the pie to safeguard this. Environmental officers stated that the pie must not lose more than two degrees of temperature during the journey. So the Yorkshire Electric Power Company supplied a control panel with graphic sensors on each part of the pie to make certain that the temperatures were maintained. For the day to be a success quite a large lot of publicity was required. The National Press were informed abut the proposed making and Frank Dale of the BBC Light Programme Tonight, came to the village to make a short film. Fife Robertson provided the commentary for the film. During the filming he was taken to The George Inn at Upper Danby to taste some of the pie taken from a 25lb 'miniature' baked by George Seville. Another event was held in Huddersfield, probably at the George Hotel, when four pies for a 'tasting' (also made by George Seville) food experts including Clement Fraud. And Phillip Harden, who agreed that the best -tasting pie was number FD 895.

The pie dish was made by Bryon Kit son at Otley; it was transported by road to Midfield and launched onto the canal. Dozes of members of the press were in attendance, together with several young female models plus several civic dignities. The dish was paddled down the canal where it was moored for the night, but overnight it unceremoniously sunk. They do say that there is no thing as bad publicity??

However a very tragic occurrence happened. Four of the top committee members were killed in a road accident. They were on the way home from London where they had been interviewed by Gammon Andrews for a TV show about the Danby Dale Pie. There names were John Schofield Haig. who was the Chairmen of the pie Committee, George Seville, who was in charge of the cook sand preparation of the pie, Lawrence Wainwright, who was the E flat double Bass player in the Danby Dale Band, he was survivor of the band that played at the pie at the 1928 festivities, ad Mr Benjamin Beaver who was the advisor to the pie committee. Mr Beaver must have been well into his eighties because he had been to the 1887, 1896 and 1928 pies. On the actual pie day the huge crown were hushed to respect these four men, falling into silence as the hymn 'Sandi' was played do honour them.

Mr Jonas Kenyon, he owner of the Fine Worsted Mill in Danby Dale, also a very well known dignitary, was the person who was given the honour of cutting the Pie. For this purpose hr had bee presented with a matching ornate knife and fork which were three foot long and had been specie commissioned fort the occasion. These probably even now still take pride of place on display in his home, next to another pair which have passed down the line in his family from previous Danby Dale pies. In 1988 a pie was made to celebrate the Bicentenary of pie making. Another was made in to celebrate the Millennium. This one wasn't huge- it wasn't enormous- it was blooming gigantic. The chap who baked this 2000 pie was Howard Gamble, this was not his first attempt at making pies, and he had baked the previous one. It was Howard 'The chief's Gamble Pie indeed. It was hoped to be a world record breaking pie, weighing in at twelve tonnes, it was forty foot long eight foot wide by forty for foot deep. It used the electricity generated to power nine homes to bake this enormous pie. Of you want to try making this at home the 'secret' recipe was.

5000 KG of prime diced quality British Beef.
2000kg potatoes , 1000oninons.
3900of water.100kg John Smihs,Best Bitter.
200kg of Beef bouillon.
mi xed herbs. ,
gravybrowning and pepper to taste,
3465kg shortcake pastry.

To Prepare.

1, have plenty of very willing helpers, 2, divide all the ingredients equally 3, haves all liquid in pie dish ready to add the meat and onions 4, bring to a tempereture of 90c ad cook gently for approximimatly 8 hours

Dicky Bird was asked to officially open the festivities. His reply was "I am looing forward to opening the festival. "I like a nice piece of pie. I think it's the oddest job I have ever been asked to do-people all over the world ask me to do things for them, but this will be special., Danby Dale Pie is renoowned thoughout the world and I am pleased to be involved with such an old tradition, especially in Millinium year" The pie was blessd by the Bisop of Wakefield, the Right Reverand Nigel McCulloch.

The first aimof this pie was to not let the Millenium pass by without being honoured in the time honoured fashion. The next aim was to continue the self-help theme of the recent pies by providing a football field in Denby Dale and refurbishing the village youth club.

Hector Buckley was undoubtedly very useful in liasing with local farmers. Overall about five hundred acres of farmland had to be used for the pie, and all associated events and car parking. The local farmers wanted a lot of assurance that they would be compensated for any trouble that the public might cause. Also bearing in mind that the rotation of crops is something farrmers must do and though the event only took a few days it would have a six month effect on some of the fields involved. A lot of people must be congratulated for their unstinting man hours and efforts that were put into bring this event to fruition. Three different plates were made to commomerate this 2000 pie, two were produced by Peter Jones. The prices were £12.50. £24 00, &£39 00, also engraved tankers, goblets and mugs were available. I will now make a prediction, the next Deby Dale pie will be celebrated in 2015 to commutate the withdrawal of all British troops from Afghanistan. Plates will be on sale of 250 Eros. Proceeds will go to PMP (Poor members of Parliaments pension's funds). I have enjoyed the research (and digging in my noodle box) for all these events, and apologise to anyone if I have made any errors with my 'facts'.

The 1877 Pie hat

Mr Jonas Kenyon, a local Mill owner cutting open the 1964 Pie.

The shop did not do as much business as the Mobile shop, by a long way; I employed my daughter Sandra very briefly in the shop. She got married on 2oth July, shortly after we moved into the shop and soon made Bessie and I grandparents. Gillian was born on14th of May 1964. Sandra's husband was George Marsh he came from Carlecotes. After their wedding they rented a small cottage opposite Kenyonns

Mill before being allocated a council bungalow, near their Grandma and Granddad Clegg. The ceremony took place at Denby Dale Perish Church in the shadows of the Denby Dale viaducts. The reception for the six bridesmaids, family and friends was at The Stanhope Arms, Dunford Bridge about 10 miles away near Calicoes. So a coach was laid on to transport every one there. When Sandra could no longer work in the shop, my other daughter Christine left school to work for me. Saturday was my busiest day on the mobile shop Christine used to come with me, when Bessie didn't have one of her frequent Saturday morning migraines. Eventually I employed my nephew Bernard Harris, one of my sister's sons. I covered a fairly large district.Denby Dale Upper and Lower, Cumuberwoth, Sovereign, Shipley, Bird sedge, Lower Danby and Dunkirk, and several outlying farms. It was long hard hours going but very financially rewarding. We only sold top quality produce, I managed to pay off my loan fairly quickly .it was in that period that I became a new car fanatic. I have had at least twenty eight different vehicles, only a few of them were second had. Well somebody had to keep the car industry going?

It is said that everyone knows where they were when JFK was assassinated; Christine and I were with our regular customers in the triangle in the Sovereign area on hat fateful evening, at about seven pm when we heard about it.

We started to get adventurous now, when it came round to the annual holiday time. Flying to Douglas, on the Isle of Man, it was Bessie and Christine's first experience of flying. We flew from Blackpool Airport and the plane was so old that it almost had to flap its wings to keep air bourn. Freddie and the Dreamers and Ivy Benson's All Girls Band were in concert there and we managed to get tickets to see them. Of cause, I'll never forget another act that we saw there. This was Johnny Peulteo and his Harmonica Rascals. Johnny was a midget and the harmonica that he played was almost was wide as he was tall. His routine was jam-packed -full of slapstick comedy. For the next two years Bessie and I enjoyed holidays on Jersey , first of all at St Helier, and then at Beaumont. What a beautiful place Jersey is. My first really good wristwatch and camera were bought in the Duty Free shop in Jersey. . Don't remember declaring them on my return home (tut tut.) We saw the 'Sound of music' and 'Mary Pupin's' whilst there.

For our second visit to Jersey we booked our package through Hansoms Travel Agency at Huddersfield. At the end of our holiday at the airport when we tried to book in for our homeward flight we were told that the flight number on our tickets was fictitious, it just did not exist. Oh Calamity. Sandra and George were picking us up from Leeds Airport, so I had to ask the check-in girl if I could ring home to stop them setting off to Leeds airport to pick us up, we caught them just in the nick of time. They were just about to leave. We were then booked in on another plane, as first reserves; if somebody did not turn up we would be able to travel. However, when it came to the time for the flight, just as we were about to walk on the tarmac and board the plane a message was given out on the tannoy system saying "Would Mr and Mrs Parkinson please report to Flight desk one" of coarse that was because everybody had turned up for the flight, which meant that was could not travel on that plane. So we rang home and told them the sorry tale. About two hours laterwe did get manage to get a plane to Manchester Airport I was about to ask the check in girl if could phone my daughter again when I suddenly realiesed that that this flight was going to arrive at Manchester in the middle of the night, and it was inconsiderate to expect Sandra and George to pick us up when they had two very young children. this 'plane was so old that it could have been flown originally by the Wright Brothers. The airline arranged for us to be picked up by taxi, at no charge. We were ushered straight through Customs.

On evening when I returned from my Greengrocers round, I went upstairs to have a wash and was shocked and amazed to find twin beds in our bedroom where our double bed usually was. Bessie had been to Beaumonts Warehouse in Huddersteld to choose these, without prior consultation with myself. We shall hear more about these beds later in the storY

I had some very good customers, and one ort three that were odd to say the least, One niggardly customer at Shipley use to ask me for such things as six potatoes and fifteen garden pea pods and the likes , it was never a pound of this or the other. Another customer asked me for two ounces of mushrooms "Threes only four of us for tea - we'll have mushrooms on toast" yet another customer who seemed quite well off asked me to cut some stalks of some mushrooms stalks, because they were cheaper than whole mushrooms, she as very taken aback because I wouldn't. (I could write a book, I thought) oh dear, silly me I am doing!! One episode on a Friday at Shepley I accidentally knocked down a wall. I think that every other tradesman in the district had must have knocked it and loosened it I just nudged it which must have put the final touches to it, and down it went. This was at nine o'clock at Friday night, next morning (Saturday) someone from the local council telephoned and asked me what was I going to do about it? On a Saturday you normally can't even get in touch with any one on a weekend. Bloody marvellous. I lord them to repair it and send me the bill. The only damage I did to my van was or put a dent in one of my mudguards. At my next customer I based my ankle on a wooden box that was jutting out and uttered an oath or two, this lady told me that "I should not swear George, because it was bloody bad manners" I have used the expression on occasion since.

I was in the greengrocery business for four years, it was a very good business but I think that I got out at the right time car ownership was looming, as were supermarkets, in fact one customer told me that as they had a car now she would not want me to call as often. Needless to say I never called again. In our fourth year year at the shop, we had booked to go to Blackpool on Holiday to Redmans Park Hotel with a mate of mine Les Brook and his wife Olga. When we received family news from Blackpool, my wif's sister had a Private Hotel there. Her husband was taken ill and they wanted to sell. Big headed I thought that I would have no problems handling the workload, if I decided to take on such a challenging venture. We looked further into it. With a small bank loan and a private loan from my wifes sister, we managed to cobble enough together to buy the property. It did ease the situation somewhat when I sold my car, a greyish blue Ford Coursair Estate car, knowing it was not essential to have a car at Blacpool. They wanted to sell up as quickly as possible. So our planned holiday with Les and Olga had to be scrapped. Very luckily I knew of a prospective buyer foot the Greengrocery business.it was Roy Hurst, who was another old workmate of mine.at Park mill Colliery. He jumped at the chance and by several minor miracles we moved into Homestead Private Hotel

57 Dean Street. Blackpool on Tuesday the fourth of July 1967. I believe we paid six thousand pounds for the establishment. I became the head cook and bottle washer , the kitchen was my domain , previously I had only cooked form family and had never had a lesson, but as previously I was a quick learner my sister in-law looked on for a couple of weeks and I soon got the hang of it. In fact would you believe me if I said I just got on with it, well same as me you have no option. We rarely bought anything ready cooked or baked. It was not easy, but I enjoyed it. I love a challenge. At the height of the season it was nearly eighteen hours a week. One amusing that did happen was shortly after we got there. I had to admit defeat on afternoon when I found that I had not enough time to do cake-baking for tea time tables. I sent Christine to the local cake shop for a couple of dozen mixed buns. she came back a bit upset and said "Dad when I asked for the buns they said they had sold out, but I could see plenty in the window "Luckily Auntie Gladys was there and laughingly told Christine that what Yorkers called buns were called cakes in Lancashire. 'Buns' were bread rolls etc in Blackpool. Strangely enough Christine was never keen to go back to that particular shop. I made everything I possibly could, because I am a tight Yorkie. But mostly it was a challenge to take on and get under my belt. One of Christine' sayings is "You can take the lass out of Yorkshire, but you can't take the Yorkshire out of the lass" (like her daddy) thereby hangs another tale when our daughter was a toddler, people frequently commented "Isn't she like her daddy", she started to anticipate what they were going today, when they looked in her pram she would say "like a daddy" I as not able to blame that on the milk man. Back to my story, we had eleven bedrooms and we were able to accommodate thirty three guests. But that was stretching it to the limit and it did not happen on many occasions. Twenty eight was a more comfortable number. We were in the centre of Gladstone Terrace of five three story Victorian purpose built boarding houses, with large 'Dry' cellars; there were hundreds of such properties in Blackpool. many of them identical. I would not say it was in poor condition when we bought it but it was a bay tired. There were a lot of things I did not like. I took out several fireplaces, some of which were cast iron, and would have been worth a bob or two now, that also applies to a lot of things we have chucked out .It took me (when I say me I mean me)about four years to get things just

as I wanted them. Even out of season I had to break off from whatever I was doing, to cook meals. I must have been crackers to put up with it.

Also at this time Fire Regulations were altered, and quite an upheaval took place. All bedroom doors had to be made fire proof, and automatic door closers fitted. And as we had no room for an outside fire escape, we had to make doorways through to the next house on each landing and install fire doors. It must have been awkward if you had an unfriendly neighbour, but luckily we were on very good terms with all our neighbours... Fire alarms had to be fitted, and apart from these. I did all the work myself. I heard about a Hotel in St Anne's that was being demolished and acquired two of the necessary fire doors from there. It was all passed on the first inspection.

Another thing I did was to alter all the beds. They were all old fashioned ones with large bed heads and bottoms. I sawed off the bottoms and made them more modern, my wife played hell about this. , but she had to admit later, that the beds were easier to make up. (Praise indeed) it also made the rooms look a lot bigger. I think that by now you will have picked up the fact that romance had evaporated in our martial status by this time.

Just before Christmas 1970 Christine started courting a coloured soldier, Greg Rutter. who was stationed at Weeton Camp. Just over a year later they were married at Waterloo Road Methodist Church. Greg had to fly over from Germany , where he had been posted. For the ceremony .We had the reception at our Hotel, Gregg's family lived in Lossiemouth in Scotland and travelled down on the previous day for the ceremony. We accommodated them in our Hotel. The next morning at Breakfast we told everyone, that we would not have the time to provide them lunch. Despite these several of them turned up expecting something. For the reception I boned and stuffed several Chickens in aspic so that they sliced and served with ease I also boiled a cow's tongue, and we had a salad with it. I made and decorated a three tier square wedding cake. instead of tins, I made some wooden ones.

I acquired this idea from a magazine, and with the cake being baked on a very low heat, there was no danger to the wood charring. The cake was a huge success; I received many compliments about it. The cake tasted as good as it looked, with no trace of crust.

For the evening entertainment we went to the Horse Shoe Bar at Blackpool Pleasure Beach. At that time Edward Heath was having a dispute with the miners. And almost all industry was on a three day week. There were lots of power cuts. We new about these in advance and bought a copious supply of candles for the Hotel. I remember walking down to the Pleasure Beach in darkness all the street lights were off. The Pleasure Beach probably had their own generator and emergency lighting, though I remember that we drank and were entertained by candlelight. That in no way interfered with the drinking abilities of several of his family, including the groom. The thanks we got from the guests were very disappointing.

A few months later, when accommodation was arranged, Christine flew out to join her new husband in Germany.

Also at this period I had three different cars, a Daf33, 750cc with an automatic gear box which was rather unique because it was belt driven. I swapped that for a Daff 55, which was similar but improved. Christine bought this from us, and then I bought a Citroen special 1200cc which was a nice car but was a sod for starting in cold weather. Even inside a garage at Blackpool it was difficult to start, at that time electronic ignition was in its infancy. Most new cars from then on were fitted with it. Unfotrunalatly I could not get a kit for that car.

Christine returned from Germany in 1973 and lived in various flats in Blackpool until 1975 when she was pregnant. About this time we heard from Sandra that the pub where she and her husband worked was for sale. I must point out at this stage, that our hotel was a good business, but it was not what you could say a real money spinner, in other words there was not a lot to spare money to look forward to retire on. Also by this time holidays aboard were beginning to take our business away. So we pricked our ears up at this information. The pub involved was The Fox house at Hade Edge a pub and restaurant near Holmfirth in Yorkshire It was a pub that I was a little familiar with. I was a bit sceptical for a start mostly because of my very limited knowledge of the pub side of the business. Also the A La Carte side was a bit different than what I was now used to. However Sandra ran the restaurant side on her own at times and her husband was familiar with the pub side. We decided to have a family confab to mull it over, and it was too good a thing to just dismiss out of hand. And decided to look into it a bit further. First of all we had our present property valued A bank manager friend arranged this free of charge. I was pleasantly surprised when it was valued at sixteen thousand pounds. We looked at the financial side of the business. And decided that it could be feasible with a bank loan plus a loan from Bass North at very low rate (2%) Bass had stimulated that we should buy all out beer from them... We didn't consider that this would be a difficulty because they did already have some Bass Beers in the pub. It was a free house. And the asking price was thirty thousand pounds. We decided that we, as a family, we could take this on. Because it was a well patronised pub and restaurant the big snag was the present owners, who did not like the restaurant side of it, and wanted to move to a pub that did not sell food. These places were and more so now, about as rare as hens teeth. they dialled and dallied so long that the loan from Bass North was no longer available, so we had to 'put it on hold' After a while this pub was sold by auction. We did go to the sale hoping! It was sold for thirty four thousand pounds. We fell out of the bidding because that was beyond our reach.

After a while my accountant , Keith Longbottom of Harris and Co at Barnsley , telephoned me and told me of another hotel and restaurant in Yorkshire that was for sale. It was the Great Western Hotel in Marsden near Huddersfield. A decent sized pub with a Fifty cover restaurant. It was in a very isolated position on the moors between Huddersfield and Oldham. And was owned by Mrs Robinson of Hade Edge. We went to see her about it and she offered me a private loan. The interest would be two per cent over the bank rate. Also I managed to get a free interest loan from three breweries that were supplying the pub at the time provided that I continued to buy beer from them. These were conditions applied to these loans, I had to provide collateral in the form of pub and restaurant furniture, it was more or less a formality. The bank rate at the time was eight per cent, in a couple of years it had escalated to fourteen per cent, people grumble profusely about the present rate. We had a lot if interest in the hotel at Blackpool, so we assumed that we would have no great difficulties in selling it. It was sold first of all to a manager of a NAAFI from Aldershot Barracks. This man was so sure that he would be able to afford it that he started 'buying' various items which I stored for him. However he had been economical with the truth, when filling in his loan form. Apart from the loan from the bank he was getting loans from two more sources. The bank would have none of this and so, the loan fell through. Then we had to start all over again and almost immediately we had several interested prospective purchasers. Eventually it was sold to a Blackpool taxi driver. So then we were able to complete the deal and move to Marsden. The whole to this business took five months and in the mean time at the start if the season we had changed from Full Board to Bed and Breakfast and evening meal. If I had realised how much easier this proved to be, and I am talking about *much* easier. I would have seriously considered staying at Blackpool.

We moved to the Great Western on the First of October1975.This was at a fairly quiet time The Great Western was what is called 'a summer pub'. Christine and Greg moved with us, she as great with child at the time (one of our customers described her as twelve months pregnant) at the time. Granddaughter Fiona arrived on the eighth of October. However relations with my son- in- law deteriorated badly. I will not elaborate on that too much one of the things that I could not tolerate was his philandering. Not very long after that they moved to Scotland, I tried not it let it bother me, it was very sad for us all. We remained estranged for a long time. My wife kept in touch by letter. Eventually they moved back into civilisation in Blackpool. And my(by then-ex -wife(who I shall tell you more about later, lived with them for twenty years between 1978- 1980. no this is not a miss print (Christine's own words 'that's' what it felt like.)The spring and summer of 1976 were extremely busy, it was scorching hot for weeks on end, and we were so busy in the pub that at times we hardly had time to dry the glasses before they were needed again. After washing them we had to put them on the shelves still wet, glass washers had not been thought about then. Environmental Officer nowadays would have kittens if they could see what we did back then. During that hot spell I recall one old fell saying to me ''I wish it would cool down all this supping is costing me a bloody fortune"

That summer was so hot and dry that stand pies were erected in many places also the moors surrounding us were on fire. Mostly set on fire by arsonist's .We bad out own water supply. Where the source of it was I do not know. It ran off the moor into a concrete tank in the back garden. It was then pumped into e very large tank in the loft. To say the water was absolutely delicious and a delight would be a gross understatement. The big snag being that it was so acid it corroded the copper pipes plus the hot water tank and the back boiler. In turn all these were replaced by stainless steel, it cost a fortune. The restaurant was also very busy. Sandra and George her husband were a godsend to me, as was my granddaughter Gillian, she was only twelve that first summer, but she could run rings round all the other girls. Mind you she was a goer she had her own two businesses when she was seventeen.

The first day at the pub was a good test for our capabilities a funeral tea had been booked for about thirty mourners. Also in the evening Saddle worth Round Table were booked in meal, followed by a good quaffing session. (They <u>could</u> sup) it was hard going, am I allowed to say it again 'we just got on with it'! We seemed to make a good impression , I had a peep at the minutes of that meeting, and it said that the meal was of a much better standard 'must be something to do with the new landlord. The Round Table's were a boon to us in the winter months because apart from them trying to drink us dry, many a time, and you know a crowd attracts a crowd, by that I mean when people se a lot of cars at a pub , they think that must be a good pub , we'll pop in there for a few swift halves. We stayed open for them until the early hours in the morning. 'Twas a mystery to me how they escaped prosecution for drink driving! Mind you we stayed open very late at week ends but as long as you didn't have any trouble the law kept a blind eye to it.

We had only been at the pub for a short time when my wife said that she was never going to like it up there and she wanted us to leave. We were very isolated up thee at 1300ftabove sea level. The nearest village was three miles away, when we looked out at night we could only see one light. And if they had gone to bed there were none. However she was well aware of all this before we bought it and had moved there. She nagged me daily about he situation, I had no intention of leaving, besides which I could not afford. She then began to have migraines on a regular basis, she decided, at a very busy time, to go and stay with some mutual friends at Clayton West for a week. Whilst she was away, to try to save our very shaky marriage, I went to a factory in Huddersfield to have a very large bed made. Six foot by six foot six inches apathetic bed. The bedding was difficult to find, but I managed to locate some before she retuned. The ordering was on the Tuesday and was delivered on Thursday a minor miracle but was determined to get it all sorted out before she got back from her 'holiday'. You see we slept in in the twin beds she had chosen without consulting me, for several years, it was not my style, but I had to put up with it. When my wife arrived back from her 'vacation' she informed me that she had been to the Doctors while she had been away. And that she had told her that she had a bad heart. That really did shake me but not for long, about half an hour later she went up stairs and saw the new bed. She went berserk with rage. And within half an hour she had dismantled the new bed taken it to another room, put it behind a heavy Victorian wardrobe and got the old beds back in our room!! So much for a weak heatr1 ho bloody ho!!! Our friends did not say anything at the time but they said never again, meaning the 'vacation'. At the time of writing she is still in pretty good form for her age 87

Shortly after this she walked out on me a couple of times. Each time I fetched her back, however things did not improve and finally she went to live with her sister Anna and her husband Eric at Danby Dale, I found out later that she had given them a pretty miserable time.

Her father the afore mentioned Basil, came to fetch her belongings. He said to me that I should be ashamed of myself because I was driving his daughter to an early grave. I simply told him that he should keep his gob shut. As he had no room to talk, after the way he treated his wife all those years ago (he had run off with a floozie at one time) I could elaborate on that for another chapter.

Around this time I thought that the restaurant was looking a bit down in the mouth, also the radiators were not very efficient I decided to give the whole entire place a revamp. I took out a fire place and chimney breast that gave us a bit more space. Then put in modern radiators, and re-carpeted it and put down a small dance floor. I did ninety pre cent of this work on my own, a very good friend. Freddie Guest helped me. To commemorate this we had a Grand Reopening, I laid on a large complimentary buffet and invited all my regular customers. Four of them sang as a Barbers Shop Quintet they were good! And they brought along an accordion player to provide some entertainment (the promise of free nosh and beer, no doubt helped!) I asked a *friend* of mine from Blackpool to do the grand reopening his name was Egroeg Nosnikrap,(spell it backwords) a rather eccentric chap. This gentleman arrived in evening dress complete with a black cape, a top hat and a silver-capped walking cane, I fooled them all it was *himself,* and I had borrowed all the clobber from Huddersfield Thespian Society Also I got a local cobbler to higher my shoes by four inches. A local actor gave me a facial makeover, with a beard and moustache I could hardly recognise meson, and I looked a proper part. All this facial decorating was done in the privacy of my bedroom. I then went out of the back door and round to the front, where my actor friend introduced me to my family. I had a small bevy, just to steady my nerves of course. Then proceeded to open the restaurant. After a few minutes I could no longer keep up the facade any longer, I took off the facial furniture and those high heeled shoes, which were the worst part of the my set up. I had great difficulty walking in them. I was really chuffed with it all, not a thing had gone wrong, I had actually pulled it off it was a real good net. an' we did sup some stuff !At the end when we had gathered the crumbs from the table I felt a bit Biblical and even considered going over the road to the reservoir to catch two small fishes to perform a miracle with the crumbs

Occasionally I would advertise in the local papers, I tried to make it amusing, the best was.

Stand edge Thirst and Hunger Clinic.

Surgeries Daily.

Diagnosis Free.

Dispensations Reasonable.

It caused quite a lot of mirth plus a god inflow of thirsty and hungry customers. One of the Daily Examiner's columnists was so amused that he wrote an article in the paper about the ingenuity of it (actually the thirst and hunger bit had been pinched from a Radio Leeds afternoon programme)

Apart from being shot at , with intention to kill, almost blowing myself and my pub to oblivion, being almost buried alive down the mine, and being almost drowned by a sudden inflow of water, several occasions with broken ribs, hitting myself in a shot firing episode, I think I may have led quite a humdrum life

Around this time I had to reluctantly change my car The Citroen 1200 Special was a good car, but it was a bad starter. Reliability was an absolute necessity for my business particularly bearing in mind that I had to fetch my staff to work, then after closing time I had to take them home again. You see the bus service which ran past the pub was practically useless. We had about six a day and the last bus was at eight pm. so I exchanged the Citroen for a Hillman Hunter Estate car. I had not that very long when. Whoops!!! I had a serious entanglement with a cow, one of the bovine varieties. You see the roads around there were unlit, also they not fenced. So the cattle and sheep roamed at will. This particular night, when returning after taking my staff home, at about eleven thirty at night. a monster of a bovine creature loomed at me ; Bang!! To quote, "I did not do much damage, just bent the bonnet and front wing, broke the windscreen, bent the right windscreen pillar , damaged the drivers door. and knoccked off the right hand mirror" (with apologies to the Norwich Union) apart from that and a face full of scratches I was honky dory!! then the beast ambled off on its merry way (just minus the one horn!)perhaps it was heading for a swift halve at the Coach and Horses and didn't know it was past closing time.

We were situated on the A62 between Huddersfield and Oldham, just below Stand edge cutting it did rain a lot and we were exposed very much to the elements, but when you live in a rain gathering district. You must expect this, a friend of mine commented once, that it was a god thing we had no trees near us, or it would never seem to stop raining, because it would be always be dripping off the branches. It wasn't that bad in fact when it was fine, the panoramic views were breathtaking, and we had an abundance of lovely fresh air. We also had a copious supply of thirsty customers, some of them who routinely visited us to practice that quaint old Yorkshire custom of getting as drunk as a skunk.

When the weather behaved it self up there it was beautiful, the downside was all that white fluffy stuff that came **every** winter and it came in prolific doses. Many were the time when we had to close because of snowdrifts and the like. The police sometimes blocked the roads off; the worst occasion was in 1978 when we were closed for the majority of the winter months. Bankruptcy loomed large, it was not just the loss of customer takings, and we also lost vast amounts of beer and lager going off. Plus we only used fresh foods. Hefty amounts of provisions had to be thrown away.

One Thursday afternoon it started snowing at about two forty five ,just as I was setting off to take Sandra home to Hade Edge , before we got halfway there we were slipping about all over the road, so I stopped to fill my boot with wall toppings from a nearby dry stone wall. (Don't try this if you have front wheel drive) then we progressed a lot better. Yes I did replace the stones. However when I got back to Marsden the police had closed the road off. And would not let me pass them. Luckily someone with a front wheel drive Land Rover came along, he lived about a mile up the road so he took me home. There was a way to by-pass the barrier but the police were watching me so I could not try it. I remember when one chap did exactly that, and he was extremely lucky to tell the tale. That evening there was a howling blizzard and my young stepdaughter said to me, Dad there is someone knocking at the door (We lived upstairs) I said no love , it will be the wind making something rattle. However she insisted that I go a look, she was right it was a man and he was only dressed in a lounge sit, he was in a terrible condition, another few minutes and he would have been a goner. We had to carry him into the pub, sit him down, and take his frozen wet clothes off. And wrap him up in warm blankets. Then we tried to get a warm drink into him. It was an extremely long time before he could even speak, eventually we managed to get him to bed with every hot water bottle we possessed. We kept looking on him and eventually he stopped shivering, then we gave him something to eat, and left him until the following morning. It tuned out that he was a pool table salesman who had been down the valley to make a sale and he was on the way home to Oldham. He had got stuck in a drift a few yards past the pub. The next morning the snow had sopped and it was a lovely day, we of course gave him his breakfast and he had telephoned the AA telling them where he was and that he had broken down. Would they come to him? I was surprised when they did and they were not very long about t either. Obviously they must have dug him out because we never saw hen or heard from him again. He went without even a word of thanks; we did not even know his name.

On another occasion a motorway maintenance van and trailer came up and could get through the cutting so they turned round and parked in front of my pub (we were closed because of the snow) they knocked on the door and demanded food and accommodation. My immediate reaction was to deny them anything "you should not have come through the barriers then you would not be in this position" I closed the door and left them to it. About an hour later my conscience struck me. (It wouldn't look good in the national press. *"Men found frozen to* death *outside a pub")* so I knocked on the Dore and there they were snug as a bug in a rug. They had a calor gas going and were busy eating bacon egg and sausages. I said god night and closed the door.

No doubt you will have noticed that I must have remarried, well I was divorced from Bessie and once more, have had another bite of the cherry.

Her name was Janice of of my barmaids; she had a young daughter Vanessa. Who I adopted immediately.

One evening (it was my night off from cooking) was nicely comfortable in my armchair when someone shouted up to tell me that I was needed in the kitchen. They were exceptionally busy, my first question was "have you some plates warming" at the same time I turned on the oven, that's where we warmed the plates. The reply was "yes" so I shut the oven door but did not turn the gas off. A few minutes later when I wanted some warm plates, I opened the oven door and the gas enfolded itself onto the lit ring on the cooker, exploded and blew me across the kitchen setting fire to my hair and in the process made me look like a red Indian. Looking back, I think that a lot of these accidents were due to over work. I was a bit of an alcoholic (Whoops, wrong word what I really meant to say was workaholic!!!) however, being self employed I had not much option, but to get on with it.

You would think that living at that height you could not get flooded. However, the drains at the top side of my pub were made up and during a big downpour some debris formed on the road at the top end of the car park, and diverted a small river into the back door. We didn't notice it for a while. , fortunately it only flooded the cellar where there were plenty of drains. But it still took some time to clean it up. Despite all these tales of woe, it was one of the happiest periods of my life.

One good source of income was 'morning drives', these were parties of men , mostly from Working Menes Clubs, who called in for breakfast , full English of course , on there way to a sports meeting isn't it wonderful how much nicer beer tastes before and after regular hours. They usually drank abundant amounts of it too! The local constabulary turned Nelsons eye to it.

One party that stands out in my memory came from Wilson' s Brewery of Manchester, (now defunct) There coach was well loaded up with bottled ale, and they had been drinkig on the way to my pub. They then had their breakfast and drank in my pub until lunchtime .Then they went to York Races. They returned that evening; just to refresh their dry throats of coarse they were talkative but no trouble at the same time in the restaurant we had a wedding anniversary party going on. One of the breakfast parties fancied himself as a vocalist. Yes you would be right in thinking that he was nicely oiled He went in to the dining room to sing for them and while he was there he told them one or two risqué jokes. They took it in all good part, and when they were leaving they gave him some of their anniversary cake. Which was wrapped in a serviette, he put it in his pocket. Just before he left he was feeling rather fragile, so he took out his false teeth wrapped them in a serviette, and put them in his pocket. And then went across to the road to the Red bank Res' to throw up his days imbibing. He didn't like fruit cake so he took it out of his pocket and threw it in the res' Next morning He put his hand in his pocket for his gnashes and lo and behold he took out "Yes you have guessed correctly" the piece of fruit cake. (Oh calamity)

He immediately returned to the reservoir and asked members of the sailing club to have a look for them. They just laughed at him, but luckily Oldham Sub Aqua club where there at the time and in my opinion he was very fortunate they obliged him and recovered them for him.

The Sub Aqua Club came to the reservoir all year round, it would have been a good exercise for them they were good customers and on occasion tried to drink us dry. Huddersfield Sub Aqua Club also came up quite a lot they came without fail on New Years Day. Many was the time when they had to break the ice with a sledge hammer (I am shivering at the very thought of it) When those who had already had their dip came across to the pub and he optics on the spirit bottles were almost seized up. Though over use. They were a good natured lot and we stayed open for them until they had their fill. There were quite a few of the constabulary amongst them

About that time, One Sunday morning, someone was knocking at the front door. My cleaning lady went to the door to see who it was. She brought in a very distraught man We say him down but he was too upset to speak. Then we gave him a drink of hot sweet tea, and after a while he was able to tell us what had distressed him. Apparently he was a member of Red Brook Sailing Club. And he had come up to do some repairs to his boat. First of all he saw something hanging from the sailing clubs chimney pot. It turned out to be a body. I then went to have a look for myself, and my first impression was that it was a hoax; I thought that it was a tailor's dummy. However on closer examination I could see that it was the body of an old man. I then sent for the police, also telling them about the condition of the man who had found him within a few minutes some one took him home. Both uniformed and plain clothed policemen arrived, at a rough guess about twenty of them. It must have been a quiet day the situation did not warrant so many (maybe because if was at a pub?) however I did not grumble as they were knocking it back a bit.

It turned out that it was the body of a Manchester bus driver whose regular route took him by the pub. The man who found the body turned out to be of a nervous disposition. he took his boat away and never retuned to Red Brook again.

About this time I divorced my wife, it was not a pleasant time and left me almost stony broke. I had no option but to get on with it, you see when she left me her passing words were "You will not last long now you will not be able to manage without me" That of course made me more determined to manage, I will be the first to admit that it was not easy, but with lots of reorganisation I did alright. She expected of course to get half of everything. Fortunately the court did not see it that way. She got a decent settlement and thirty two pounds a week allowance. Which considerably dinted my finances .About five years later she took me to court to get a better allowance? I was by then remarried and I had adopted a young child. I produced accounts showing that I could not afford any increase in her allowance. She had done me a big favour, the recorder lowered he allowance to eighteen pounds a week, and also stipulated that this would cease when I reached retirement age. I can see the expression on her face mow. Well she went for a better allowance, it certainly was better for me.

Another thing happened, I was burgled at the time, when the only living companions were my Lakeland terrier Bobby, and his bite was worse than his bark. One Sunday afternoon I arrived back from taking my staff home, quite a bit larger than usual I was offered cup of tea at last drop off. The first thing I noticed was the charity bottle had been broken and the coins scattered all over he place. The notes of which they had been plenty were of coarse gone. Then I noticed the broken window. Any how he had a very good haul we'd had a very good lunch time both in the restaurant and in the pub about £400 plus what he took from the bottle. What a mess he had made all the drawers and cupboards emptied, I was lucky in one thing I had a tattered old handbag in one if the cupboards with quite a deal of 'contingency' money. he had pulled that out but not looked inside it. My dog was at the back of the sofa shaking like a leaf Don't know what he did to him. I did get compensation from my insurance, the man who did it was a Pakistan from Liverpool he was caught in Birmingham and asked of 20 others cases to be taken into consideration

Another queer story now. Manchester United were playing a mid week evening match some where in Yorkshire, and the police rang me up to inform me that the fans would be travelling back past my pub, well we all know what they can be like, any how the police could not spare any men to cover me and they advised me to close my pub at 9.00pm. Well what I did was put out all outside lights pull the curtains and dim the lights in the pub and lock the door letting in only people that I knew. I thought that I had taken care of all the risk. However a young man whose name was David Airedale, came up to the pub abort half past ten for his usual drink. Now this bloke had a First Class Degree with Honours in lying, When he saw the lights off he turned round and went down to a village pub.

Next morning when I went for my newspaper , as soon as I entered the shop , thee newsagent and his wife went ashen, the lady came round the counter and gave me a hug (which I enjoyed) and sat me down , I said to them "what ever is the matter, you both look as if you have seen a Ghost" They both chorused "you could not be nearer to the truth" it was running round the village that I was dead Gossip in a village spreads like a forest fire. to say that I was shocked was an understatement they made me a good cup of that resurrection stuff otherwise known as hot sweet tea. Then I went off to find the source of the lie. It did not take long to find the culprit it was the aforementioned David Airedale. Apparently he had told the landlord of the Junction Inn on the previous evening that I had passed away. I immediately went to his home and he was not in, I told his father to pass the message to his son to keep out of my way unless he wanted some very rough treatment. Thankfully I never saw him again.

Now I have a really strange story to tell, it came about one very foggy evening when a helicopter pilot got lost somewhere on the moors near to the Great Western. Apparently he got lost and was running out of fuel so he just put it down where he could , abandoned the chopper and didn't report it to the police , and legged it home (I am told that this is a mere six miles or so across a very boggy moor- in fog!!) Yeah, sounds really likely doesn't it. THis first thing I knew about this was next morning after collecting my cleaners from Marsden. The moor just below me was swarming with people. Some were in police uniform, many were not. I thought that some kind of exercise was going on; A while later a long flat bottomed lorry appeared in my car park. The driver told me that he had come to collect a helicopter. Soon after this we heard the sound of a helicopter overhead when it appeared it had another helicopter dangling beneath it. I have a photograph of this or

I may not believe it. Apparently what had happened another plane had spotted the copter on the moor and thought it had crashed? That was the reason for all those people on the moor apart from that I think that there would be another side to the story.

In 1978 I got entangled again with the Female Fatale when I engaged in Holy Matrimony once more; you have got to admit that I'm a trier. I have also been told on occasion that I am trying. I married one of my staff and for thirteen years I thought that we were reasonably happy.

During this period I had another series of accidents. First of all I thought that I could try a spot of tap dancing. One morning when cleaning the tiles over the kitchen sink I slipped off the sink and demolished a pair of wooden steps that I had used to climb onto the sink. I was knocked out and broke several ribs. I can assure you that some things diminish with age but pain is not one of them I had hardly recovered from that when I was fetching a bucket of coal in from outside , on a very frosty night when I slipped and fell onto the bucket and cracked some mote ribs.

I could possibly go down in the history books as being something of a 'freak' in the Licensed Victualler trade I was a very light drinker. All that changed one New Years Eve night I got close and personal with a bottle of Rum, I kept pouring another and another and another , almost ad Infinitum or should that be ad nauseam. Eventually the forty ounce bottle was exhausted, so was I. If I say I was rough next morning that would surely would have been an understatement

I have no recollection of how my staff got home the previous night. The only thing certain was that I had to drag my aching body out of bed and drive down to Mars den to pick up those staff that was on duty for New Years Day. My wife didn't drive, so there was no other option. So I set off knowing that I would have to throw up every few minutes., I wedged a small bucket between my legs , as soon as I got back I went straight to bed and stayed there for the best part of the day. This was the time when I realised that nobody is indispensable (my staff managed quite well without me!!) January the first was always busy both in the pub and the restaurant.

Unfortunately many people were in the habit of driving up to the nearby moors and abandoning their dogs. Many was the time when I took pooches down to Slaithwaite Police Station, eventually the Sergeant got used to me going and we got quite friendly.

There was one beautiful Golden Labrador who became one of our family. He had been wandering across from the 'Res to my pub for a few days, my wife had tried to tempt him with goodies on several occasions, eventually he succumbed to the temptation of a tit bit, which helped her to coax him into the pub. Where he demolished two large tins of dog meat in quick succession. This resulted in him falling asleep in front of the fire for several hours. When my daughter came home from school she fell in love with him, if dogs can think, then he must have been thinking "I've got it made here"

I can never understand how people could abandon their four legged friends with such callous abandon. When they are taken to the Police Station, they only get two day's grace, and then they are put down. There was no way on earth that I could possibly take this lovely creature to this fate, so we christened him Sandy. I took him down to the local vet who told us that he was about tree years old, and gave him a clean bill of health. (And some worms tablets). Sandy was a bit scrawny but with lots of TLC he soon filled out and became a very god looking dog unfortunately he was very loose haired, we tried all kinds of remedies to no avail. A local chemist gave us some out of date cod liver oil (he loved it) but it did no good.

My daughter used to tease him with sweets, she would place a toffee on his nose, and point a finger at him and say "no" until the carpet was wet because of his drooling. Then she would say "OK' and he would eat it. We did not let her to do it very often.

One Sunday evening in the middle of winter he accidentally got out of the pub. And wondered onto the very boggy moor. It was pitch black so I took a torch with me and kept shouting for him. At last I heard him barking and eventually located him. We were both very lucky not to have been bogged down in the peat .Both of us were wet through and covered in wet peat and very glad to get indoors, I went in the shower with all my clothes on and poor Sandy had to hose down in the cellar.

My lovely Golden Labrador, please take me for a walk!

We also had a black poodle at the time Whisky was his name. Plus a tom cat called Ambrose. When I took the dogs for a walk Ambrose followed on. One afternoon, Sandy was asleep on the rug in front of the fire, curled up inside him was Whisky, and curled up inside the poodle was Ambrose. Mani's the timer since I wish I had taken a photograph of them. In fact I wish I had taken more interest in photography I could have illustrated. This story to better effect. By the way Ambrose was a stray (Not surprised are you?) Another dog episode was when a big fat Welch Corgi was found wandering about in the main road in front of the pub it was lucky that it did not get knocked down, some one brought it into the pub. This indeed was different, it had pearl buttons stitched over its eyes.(I am not joking) anyhow took it to the Police Station and neither of us could think of a reason for the peal buttons , he said he'd take it home with him, before putting it on records. It transpired that that the dog belonged to lady form Manchester. Her car had been stolen with the dog fast asleep on the back seat the culprits must have noticed the dog as they were passing the Great Western, and then decided to chuck it out of the car. They then drove on to near Leeds and abandoned and torched it. The lady came to the pub to thank me; unfortunately I was out when she called, so I never got to know the story about the pearl buttons. She asked my staff what my tipple was and left a tanner for me to buy myself a bottle I put the money in the charity bottle on the bar.

Another Manchester football club befell us one Saturday evening. We were inundated with City fans, the majority of them were alright. But some of them managed to sneak into the restaurant and got three large Bilberry pies. Which they proceeded to decorate the lounge with. We were so busy that this was not noticed until they had gone. What a mess , bilberries stain permanently so we had to redecorate.

The pub was very close to the Pennine Way. So we got a lot of hikers calling to rest their weary bones and refresh their dry throats. At times they did this too copiously and had to stay overnight. We were able to accommodate one or two inn the pub. The rest had to erect their Wig Wams in the back garden. We allowed them to do so FOC. I had a notice outside the pub requesting them to remove their footwear before entering the premises. The chief reason for this was because the wet peat that was adhered to them, stained the carpet so badly that it could not be removed. Mostly they were very nice people and were good customers. Odd ones did try to abuse our facilities, such as bringing their cooking utensils into the pub to clean them. On lady asked the kitchen staff to wash them. Another girl knocked at the door in the middle of the night and demanded to use to toilets, I asked her what she did when she was walking across the moor and suggested that she did the same now. Closed the door and went back to bed.

Another nasty episode betook us, in a field just below us Hells Angels were camping. On the Saturday night they decided to use our pub for a rubbish dump. They are appropriately named they were worse than animals and I was powerless to control them. I was afraid for both my family and my staff. They were drinking beer and then spouting it out over each other. Also pouring beer over each others heads. That night I closed at eleven on the dot. I would have closed earlier but I probably would have caused more trouble thy stole almost everything that was not screwed down, beer mats, beer towels, toilet rolls. Ash trays. Pictures from the wall, even an Antique window lamp. plus about eighty glasses, most of them broken outside the door. It was well into the morning hours before my wife and I had made the pub look decent again. We had to fetch a refuse bin in to put the entire rubbish in. to make things worse they had brought some of their own drinks into the pub; the place reeked of stale ale.

I had words with the owner of the field (he was a regular customer) I told him if he was stupid enough to let them come again to let me know I would keep my pub closed that night.

I must mention this, late one Friday evening the local jobs pulled down the Iron railings around the graveyard of the Clone Valley Cathedral (that is what Mars den Church is known as locally) When my friend Douglas Dixon saw them being replaced he remarked "I Do' not know why they are doing that nobody wants to get in, and I'm bloody sure that nobody is going to get out"

Alma Dixon his wife was one of my staff. She was an absolute gem to me the whole time I was there. She never let me down, except for the occasional day off for illness, and of course that fluffy white stuff that we got in prolific proportions.

Doggie and Alma also looked after my pub went I went on holiday they were very good friends and I could trust them implicitly. It was very comforting to have such good friends. At different times I employed two of their daughters Margaret and Jennifer. Just as nowadays it was difficult to get people to work unsocial hours. I employed quite a lot of different people during my stay there.

You would think with all this bellyaching that I did not have such a good time at the pub. You could not be more wrong. They were some of the best days of my life. The unpleasant things that I have mentioned were greatly outweighed by the good ones.

Once more I got the wanderlust; I was getting a bit cheesed off by the inclement weather up yonder. Several times I dare not fetch my staff up to the pub because of how the weather could clamp down. I was afraid that they may be stranded whilst up there, on occasions it did happen and they had to stay overnight. It never happened when I was single or maybe I would have struck lucky.

We started looking for a new business, and soon found one in a nearby village. We were to become Go-cart Lillis as the locals were called. As previously mentioned all villages had a nickname. Mars den people were called Cuckoos, Slaithwaite were called Moonrackers, and Linthwaite were lifters.

The business that we saw was a general store witch sold, apart from groceries, every thing that was perishable, such as flowers, fish, cream milk, bread and cakes and several other things. It was to give us a living nothing more.

Sorry I have gone off my story again, I shall have to have my legs slapped. We then had to put the pub on the market, fortunately we had it valued recently by Christies the national firm of auctioneers. So we put it on there books, it was sold the same day to a couple from a nearby village. A Mr and Mrs Sweepstake, before long to be called sheep hits, (oh dear) she was born locally and he was a Dutchman. It he was a good example of someone from Holland, and then I do not wish to come across a bad one.

I have come across many 'Tony's in my life, but he took the biscuit.

My definition of a 'Tony' is 'Tony bugger that knows owt'

That I told him about my pub and the Licensing Trade attracted only one standard reply "No problem" He *knew* he knew everything.

I was to find out later exactly what his problem was. It was pints and chasers both lunchtime and at night. He did not last very long before he did a moonlight flit, leaving behind all his furniture and a trail of depots.

Unfortunately, quite a few of the Golcar people had a severe dose of the English disease. I.e. they not like to see local people getting on. One kind young lady said to me when she was purchasing one Mars bar "this will help you to buy your next new car"

Across the road from me was the local Co-op store, because of the size if their shop and the bargaining power for bulk buying, they could offer better prices on the provision side. I could hold my own on the greengrocery side. Fish, plants and flowers as well. I thought that my perishable produce was of much better and fresher quality. However we kept our heads above water and we managed to make a living out of it.

Diagonally across from our shop lived two young ladies who decided to set up their own 'knocking shop'. They installed subdued red lighting in their lounge, and used to sit in the window, the local youth had a whale of a time.

One afternoon this was being discussed by some of my customers. The vicar's wife came in during the proceedings; she caught the drift of the conversation. And when the shop emptied she asked me what she had missed. I explained to her and she said "my word I shall have to cut down Andrew's spending money" Andrew was her husband. PC plod soon put a stop to it.

It was while at Golcar that we started caravanning. First of all we bought a second hand two wheeled caravan, it got us going, almost literally. On one of our first outings we were going on holiday to Anglesey. It was a very windy day, and what with the combination of no stabiliser, bad loading and different tyre pressures we almost were knocking at the pearly gates. I just about lost control while we were on the M62 close to Scamander Dam. The wind caught hold of the caravan and it started dancing from one wheel to the other, how I managed to regain control is a mystery to me. It was one of the first outings I had hitched up to a caravan and it would have been the last if there had been an option of turning round and going home. However this option was not available so I had to carry on. How I had regained control was a miracle, but after crises- crossing the motorway a couple of times I pulled upon the hard shoulder about a foot away from a very large lamppost. It was a very hairy experience, we carried on gingerly and as the miles went by I gained more confidence and resumed a more normal speed. A while later I pulled up on the hard shoulder because of a call of nature. We had hardly come to a stop when a traffic cop pulled up and wanted to know what the problem was. When I explained why I had stopped, he told me to hurry up with it. I opened the van door and it looked like a busy day at an abattoir, what a mess, my wife had insisted on taking a lot of provisions in the cupboards. A small bottle of tomato sauce had made a dash for it from the top cupboard whist I was doing the Lambeth walk earlier on. In all honesty it looked more like a gallon bottle. PC plod told me we could not stay there to clean it up. I was to make haste and get on my way. We were soon on our way, had a great holiday and while there I had a stabiliser fitted, so on our return journey I felt a lot more confident. Not long after that we bought a Swift 55 twin axle caravan. Which was a lot more stable than the single axle ones? More very enjoyable holidays followed in Grassington, North Yorkshire, the New Forest and Ilfracombe in Devon.

In between we found a site at Sutton in the Forest near York It was called Goose Wood, and we left it there the biggest part of the year and went to it most weekends. We could get there in an hour from our shop. When we got this caravan it caused quite a few caustic comments in the village. So we did not park it in the front of the shop even though we had plenty of room for it, we found a place at Slaithwaite where we could park if for the winter. At Goose Wood we made a few good friends, one couple in particular were Ida and Derek Mitchell Derek was and is a tribute to the National Health Service. He is a living miracle. He had been head cook at Dewsbury Hospital and had to retire early due to heart trouble. He has been in and out of many and various hospitals like a you. He has had a triple heart by-pass plus many and varied heart complaints and procedures. We have jested with him on many occasions that he is conducting a hospital food survey. If anyone can give a true account of the state of hospital food Derek is your man. All this has slowed him down somewhat, but at times I have seen him working like a navvy. He is lucky not to have 'bought' it a time or three, we had some very good times there the surrounding districts were very interesting and we got to know York pretty well. That is a very interesting and educational place, with oodles and oodles of history.

Or caravan was stolen from Goose Wood. It transpired that the owner of the site was moving it from our chosen site on to some gravel just by a gate that was only fastened by a piece of rope. He moved it to keep his precious grass in pristine condition. Apparently he had been doing this for a long time, and he would return it to its rightful place just before we were due to get back each weekend. We went to our solicitor to see what we could do about it, he advised us not to claim from the site owner as in his opinion it would be a long and protracted case with no guarantee of a good outcome, so we claimed from our insurance company. I wish I could say that this was a straightforward procedure, but I would be lying if I did. It was like knitting with fog. The caravan and contents were worth in excess of £9000. First of all the loss adjuster offered us£6000. We finally settled for £8000 and we had to fight tooth and nail for that. The manager of the Halifax Building Society who we got our insurance from helped us considerably at the time.

The police informed us that the culprit had been arrested. It turned out to be a professional thief he was from Denmark. They apparently trapped him when he tried to steal an outboard motor from a garage. He confessed to stealing my caravan and selling it to some Gypsies at Newark for the princely sum of £700 and as the caravan and the contents were valued at £ 9500 it was a good deal all around. Not bad for a night's work. I would have loved to tell the police not to find it; instead I just had to hope that it would not be found. The truth was I did not want it back after the Gypsies had used it.

It was not just the caravan; there was also a hell of a lot of good clothes belonging to my clothes fanatic wife. Also there was a full sized awning and three new bikes, plus a large amount of canned food.

After that we decided that as we used the caravan so much we would be better off moving to a different site because of the bad blood that existed between us, we would never be comfortable there again. We moved to Alperton Park near Knaresborough our friends had found the site, and they moved with us. This was a lovely mixed site of mobiles and static's and had not been overdeveloped. We were able to choose our own site on a new section of the site that had just started to develop, it was called the top field and we had full services. We were the second static caravan sited there, the first one was a retired policeman from Cleethorpes we got friendly but did not live in each other's pockets. It was the end of the season when we bought it, so we did not visit the site until the following season. The security was almost non-existent, so decided to install my own alarm system and lo and behold, the site was broken into. My caravan was entered, we had not left a lot of possessions there, and the only thing that was stolen was the alarm bell from the system. Several other vans were ransacked and a number of items were stolen, the owner of the site told us that they were installing security. It would be an infra red system and even if the owner was three miles away it would tell him if someone was breaking into the site, what a load of bullshit not a thing happened.

The warden and her husband moved and things went from bad to worse. a new warden was employed and hr turned out to be considerably worse than the previous, he was regularly 'under the weather' I saw him and the owner drinking whisky from tumblers in the warden's office, they both lost there driving licences due to the demon drink, if I were to ask you what they did to celebrate the day they got their licences back - you would not say a pub crawl now would you. You could not make it up could you? They took the car to York ten miles away and went for a pub crawl. The site went from bad to worse; there was litter all over the place. And the toilet facilities were filthy, this did not bother us too much because we had our own facilities, but it was not very nice. The rent for the site included electricity but we were severely restricted to five amps. This meant that we had to get low powered kettles and had to be careful not to have too many appliances on at the same time. or the fuse tripped and we had to pay to be reconnected, however I soon found a way round that, I knew some one who was a City and Guilds electrician and he adjusted things so that we could have thirteen amps

Let me tell you a funny story it came about when there was a very cold spell of weather. This meant that the we had used a large amount of electricity, as did other residents. I suspect that other residents had been using much the same devious part of their brains as *him;* the postman delivered a spectacularly high electricity bill to the owner of the sire. So he and the warden in their befuddled minds. Were creeping around at night looking under caravans for leaks!!! (I kid you not!!)After this meters were installed that meant (no more fiddling.)

Shortly after that we decided to close the shop but remain living in the upstairs accommodation you see a couple if factories had closed down, which greatly reduced our sandwich and snacks trade, the co-op across the road, was now open from eight to eight, and the advent of the Super market one stop shopping was biting deeply, keeping things in date was a head ache too. The hours that we had to put in to make a pittance did not compare well with the remuneration. We did not wish to go to the wall as was the way of numerous other village shops. so had a sale at reduced prices (well swooped on by the village vultures. then we just finished trading, we had no trouble disposing the shop fittings, they were modern and in good condition. we had the premises professionally assessed to see how much rental we could charge, before long we let it to two local couples who started a video rental shop it was a good step for us financially (and we had no work to do to draw in the rent.)

Unfortunately the English Disease reared its ugly head again the couples only lasted a couple of years. The Golcar Lilies preferred to travel further field to rent their videos than frequent the local outfit. It was quite sickening; really this was the worst outbreak of the disease that I have ever come across.

We then went on a conducted tour of Egypt, somewhere I have wanted to visit all my life. Our flight from Heathrow was delayed for an hour because the navigator got lost in London! That fair gave us some confidence in his mid-air navigation abilities; thankfully the flight was blissfully without incident. On arrival at Cairo Airport we were faced with wall to wall Egyptian salesmen selling Donkeys, Camels. Pyramids. And sand and every thing else. But the one that stands out was the one that was selling bottled water. . A wag that was travelling with us said , "Well its only water from the river Nile (which at that point looks filthy) he's been and bottled it this morning" I bought some and guess what it said on the bottle -yes ,' Bottled from the river Nile'!! We stayed in a hotel in the shade of the Pyramids at Giza. While their traditional Egyptian wedding took place. The courier gave us a running commentary, there were snake charmers galore and belly dances and hula hoops aplenty goodness me, and I've never seen so many hoops being twirled around so many different body parts!

I enjoyed the Wonders of Egypt like thousands before me, my observations were? "How the hell did they do it."? At every turn there was yet another marvel, the exception was the food. There was nothing wrong with the hotel food that was lovely. However we went to a Nomads tent where an Arabic meal was laid on. The only thing that

I recognised were some scrawny chicken legs, I sampled almost every thing but a few hours later on a train to Luxor 'it' (the deli belly) struck. I wanted to curl up and die. I went to the toilet so often that I ran out of bum fodder (fodder bun) so I went to ask the attendant for some He shrugged ("no comprehend") and I started to undo my trousers as if to do it there and then. Like a flash of lightening he produced some toilet paper. I was a few degrees under or couple of days, so I did not see all the wonders of Luxor. I did recover enough to cross the Nile on a Felucca to visit the Valley of Kings, and of course the Tomb of the Boy King TOOT AND COME IN? Many people will have seen this and other things about Egypt on television. Believe me, it compares badly with the real thing, the entrance and the tunnel leading to the Tomb is fabulous, it could not have been better constructed with modern equipment. The salesmen in Egypt are very persistent, if nothing else, and one of these characters, just after crossing the Nile, tried to sell me a black scarab. Naturally I could not release my tight Yorker ways so easily, so I haggled with him. This was still carrying on even when the coach was about to get underway to the valley ,even when the tour guide was chucking him off the coach did not deter him. When we reached our destination -Cur blump, there he was waiting for me. Sheer persistence paid off for him that day. I bought the Scarab and did that little boys face beam. They are truly disappointed if you don't haggle with them.

From there we went to Aswan. First of all we went to look at the famous Dam that was quite wonderful. Then we went to look at Hydro Electric power station below. It was built by Russian engineers for some political reason that did no mature, however it was a credit to them. I would have liked to have to visit the temples of Abu Simmer, but time would not allow it. We got friendly with a couple from Batley who were seasoned Egyptian travellers. We went on an educational tour of the country side on a horse and open carriage!! Our noses became well and truly educated when we came across a dead cow in the middle of the road at one point. As we could not get past it, the driver had to get down and move it. He then asked if we would like to visit his cousin's shop. (They have all got a cousin with a shop) We went there and I saw a really beautiful coffee set on a tray. I started to haggle for it. He had some kind of a speaker blaring away in the back ground and I said to my friend "what the hell is that racket" He replied "For Christ's sake shut up, or you will get us all thrown into the clink, that is someone reciting the Koran" Whoops!!! (I carried on with my haggling again)

We decided to fly back to Cairo; I could not face that long train journey again. We were put in the Hilton Hotel for the night, it was extremely luxurious and we had a good shufti round before we left, we asked someone if we could go up onto the roof someone escorted us up there. We had a magnificent panoramic view of Cairo and the Nile. I'll never forget that. Next morning we went by taxi, to rejoin our party at Giza. This was almost as hazardous as any of my wartime escapades the driver sped like a demented lunatic when I remonstrated with him he just grinned. And he took us around many unnecessary roads in order to boost up the fare, I haggled with him and got it lowered we the did the whole tourist thing of visiting all the highlights of Cairo. First of all we saw the Mosque of Mohammad Ali, witch was quite breath taking, I cannot begin to describe the opulence. You will have to go to see it for yourself to really appreciate it. Then something quite bizarre occurred. I got lost in the Old Bazaar at Cairo (Not very original eh) Apparently it is quite easy to get lost there,, many have done it before and probably many after me , then we went to the Cairo Museum , there are not enough adjectives to describe this it was stupendous. One could stay there for a month and still not take it all in.

Next day home to the shivers, it was late November, we all finished up with a nasty cold, mind you have you ever had a nice one. Just for fun a lot of little beasties had decided to have a nibble at me in the 'plane and I was covered in angry spots for a while, the things that you have to suffer for pleasure.

Shortly after this my wife got a job as a barmaid at a pub about three miles away. Our marriage had started, a while ago, to come apart. I could not understand why, also I could not comprehend why she wanted to take a barmaids job with the unsociable hours that this entailed. She could easily have got a job with better hours; it was not because we were on our uppers. I was at my wits' end.

On Christmas Eve I plucked up the courage to ask her "is there was another man involved" The reply was that there was another man, and she was deeply in love with him, plus the bombshell that she was leaving me that day! To say I was devastated would be an understatement. I will not elaborate on this it is still too painful. She also told me that she had never properly loved me. That made me think, several people told me afterwards that she had taken me on, just as a milt cow just to get what she could. By piecing things together I found out that it was an old flame that she had caught up with, and she had got the job as a barmaid so that they could meet at the pub and do their courting.I had been taking her to the pub every evening for her to carry on with her boyfriend.

After a protracted divorce which was similar to a Spanish holiday (It Costa plenty) I decided that the fair sex are not little dears, they are bloody expensive.

However eventually I drew a line under it and got on with my humdrum life. At that time the caravan site was closed, when it reopened I spent most of my time there. Eventually I bought a bigger van. The biggest that was available at the time it was like a small bungalow, it was thirty six feet long and twelve foot wide. With a fair sized lounge a nicely appointed kitchen two bedrooms and a bathroom and a separate shower. I had central heating installed (Caldor Gas) I enquired from British Telecom, if I could have a telephone installed? Before long half of the vans on the site had a telephone line. As the owner had a greedy payphone in the laundry room he must have been miffed at all these new telephones

My first static caravan

My lovely Bungalow.

The site was granted a licence to be open eleven months of the year this was when I decided to sell up at Golcar , and make the caravan main home the month that it was closed I spent with my daughter at Blackpool.

My friends Ida and Derek considered living there, but decided against it and divided their time between there and their house at Dewsbury. Before long quite a few were living on the site.

At times I was a bit lonely there, I would not call myself a loner, but I am not bored with my own company. There were always a lot of people about at the weekends. Also at the time I was very interested in and doing a lot of sketching and painting mostly water colours and crayons. Unfortunately my hand is not steady enough to do it now. My witting is bad enough and some of it resembles the passage of a drunken spider sashaying across the paper. It is much easier to use my computer to write on. The computing for idiot's course that I attended in the Reading Room at Youlgrave has finally paid off. It just shows that you can learn old dog's new tricks.

Back to my story. I lived on the site for a few years; when I badly broke my left ankle it did not completely put me out of action, because I had an automatic car. It was a bit difficult, but who the hell said that life had to be easy, I got no help from the so called warden, he was seldom on the site. And when he was, he was sleeping off whatever he had been indulging in. I did get a lot of help from one or two of the neighbours. two good friends of mine who lived a couple of vans away took my adorable monster Jake the West highland Terrier for his constitutionals Ida and Deck did whatever they could do for me, I could not have managed without them About the others those offered no help as Derek's favourite saying was "bugger me George" One bloke next door asked me to do some shopping for him. Cheeky sod. I told him what to do, but you won't be surprised to hear the next bit . Yes I just got on with it.

About this time my granddaughter Gillian Bought a house in Conisborough near Doncaster. It was a good solid building but very old fashioned I suspect that very little had been done to the property since it was built in the sixties. I spent several weeks there helping them to renovate it. I was in my element. Mr Paul Kelsall, Gillian's future husband was named by me The Clerk of Works. We worked very well together. Two fires and one complete chimney breast were annihilated. However the neighbours put up with the noise I shall never know. One thingies admired about Paul. That in consideration for the neighbours he insisted that all knocking stopped at eight thirty in the evening. Also he insisted that we made it reasonably tidy at the end of each day. That was a very good thing. I spent the better part of three days scrapping the varnished wallpaper off the kitchen walls it was stuck like the proverbial excreta to the blanket. When Paul came in that evening and saw the really badly cracked walls he decided to knock the plaster off the walls and have it re plastered, I could have wept. Paul was a fully qualified electrician and he completely rewired the entire house, another noisy filthy job. Paul's father Harold was also mucking in as much as he could, when it came to putting coving up we found that he was a nap hand at it. The whole job was long and protracted. Gillian by then was getting heavily pregnant and getting a bit shot of patience with the slow progress of the work. She cane to me one day and asked me if it was possible to finish just one room so that she could see the light at the end of the tunnel. Harold and I proceeded to finish the bathroom. When Harold was putting up the first piece of coving he cut it at the wrong angle. In my time I have heard and used the whole gamut of swear words, but Harold went on and on for about five minutes without a single repetition. We did soon get that room finished. Things slowly fell into place and we got the house habitable. During all this time for four days a week, from Monday to Thursday I camped out on site. Then I went back to my caravan to clean up and recover. I had to rough it a bit, I slept on a garden longer, and my only cooking facilities were a camping stove a frying pan and an electric kettle. I have suffered worse so I just got on with it.

Shortly after this Gillian and Paul's first child was born in Doncaster Royal Infirmary. The nurses there soon found out that something was seriously wrong with the babe's heart. Mother and son were rushed by police escort to Killing beck Hospital in Leeds. The following day we christened him Adam Paul, and shortly after that he had a thirteen hour open heart procedure. Thankfully this was a complete success and all he has to show for it nowadays is a thin very faint scar running down his sternum He has just had his eighteenth birthday he' s six foot and fit as a fiddle.

Shortly after this Gillian lost a baby son due to stillborn, in her late teens Gillian ran her own business a Bread cake and sandwich shop at Kirkby near Huddersfield. She also did mass outside catering. And helped her parents run a breakfast canteen at David Browns Gears at Lockwood

It was at this time that she met up with Andy and John (who I shall mention later).who ran the canteen at Huddersfield Cattle Market.

Sandra and George then took over the White Greyhound at Ellington near Doncaster, This was a big thriving pub and restaurant until Thatcher Heseltine and Co closed all the coal mines around them. Gillian and Andy and John moved to the new business with them. Andy was the chef and John was the chief barman. After abut eight years the whole shebang progressed to Derbyshire, where they now run the George Hotel in Youlgrave. Andy and John now have a pub in East Yorkshire.

Stephen my Grandson is married and has two boys Aiden and George they live in Youlgrave both he and his wife work at the pub, Stephen is in charge of the kitchen and dictates the extensive menu. , actually he is a butcher by trade and this stands him in good stead , they are able to buy whole carcases of meat , and little or nothing goes to waste he cures his own ham and bacon and makes his own Black Pudding(yum yum) the saliva is down to my elbow at the thought of it. Also he makes pork pies and occasionally several unusual kinds of sausages. And beef burgers, very little prepared food is bought. For the size of the place they have a very extensive menu.

Shortly after helping Gillian to renovate her new abode I started to get disillusioned with the antics of the warden and the owner of the caravan site, we had several disagreements. Because of my outspoken feelings on how the site was deteriorating. Also I began to realise that I was a long way from any of my relatives, my nearest one was fifty miles away. Any I had a bad attack of Bronchitis and that persuaded me to put my thinking cap on. I discussed this with my daughter Christine. She lived at Blackpool. And by mutual agreement I went to live there I advertised my caravan the warden offered me £1200 for it which was an abysmal offer. I had to advertise it again and eventually I sold it for £17000.

So once again was living by the sea. I am sure that my daughter welcomed me more than my son- in law Gregory did. Once he called mar a tight Yorkie. My revenge was sweet. Fiona my granddaughter was learning to drive and she lost one of her learner plates. He scoured local shops to buy just one, of course without success. I went out and bought a pack of six, he was a Scot so you will no doubt what I called him. Christine was not at all well. She had been diagnosed with the debilitating disease of ME most of the time she looked and felt Knackered. She did not get the support she desperately needed, either from hr husband or her daughter. After I had been there about twelve months he accosted me with some very nasty language, told me to get out, and threatened to beat me up. He turned very aggressive and started to take down my collection of Danby Dale Pie Plates. Christine sent for the Police who arrived quickly and soon dressed him down. And told him to behave or? What he was going to do with the plates I do not know. They are worth quite a bob or two, but only on the right market. In Blackpool he would have only got a pittance for them. Shortly after this he told Christine that he was moving out. , so she consulted a solicitor. Under his advise she stopped preparing meals for him and doing has laundry. The kitchen was a foreign land to him, so every night he would arrive home laden with food from various take away establishments. It was not long before he moved out.

Before Christine's legal aid came through, she received divorce papers from her estranged husband. Cheeky sod only said he wanted a divorce from her because of her unreasonable 'behaviour i.e. becoming ill' and so unable to do her housework, and look after him in the way that he was accustomed. If I had thought previously my divorces had been nasty, well Christine's could well be described as acrimonious.

During Christine's divorce proceedings she placed an advert in the local library for ladies to join a friendship group. From this she made some very good friends, these included Loraine, who had lost her husband from bowel cancer, and Jacqui who was widowed very young, with two young sons to bring up alone. both had lovely bubbly personalities, we all missed Jacqui when she went to live at Bournemouth if I had been the same age as her , I would have thrown my cap at her she would probably have thrown it back. We were good friends and I took her to the Grand Theatre in Blackpool to see the Swan Lake and Nutcracker Suite opera's. She recently remarried and now lives in Dubai. On a recent visit o the UK she spent a lovely afternoon with us, reminiscing and catching up with the gossip. It's obvious that she is very happy but a bit homesick.

Three months after her divorce Christine had a MRI scan, which revealed a massive brain tumour. We were both devastated. It was not very long before she was admitted to Preston Royal Hospital for a biopsy. She was in there for a few days when the consultant told her that the tumour was large and tucked away in the centre of her brain, it was benign and she would have to go home and learn to live with it.

However her condition deteriorated and her GP sent her to Blackpool Victoria Hospital for another scan which showed the tumour was continuing to grow, so she was admitted to Preston Royal again. Mr Davies was her surgeon, he performed a seven a half operation, hopefully removing every trace of the tumour, which he described as being the size of a large plum or a small apple. As they could not guarantee to have removed it all, she will never be discharged from Mr Davis's care. When he retires, she will be handed on to his successor. She was told that they had removed it in the nick of time or it would have blinded or paralysed her. A sobering thought indeed.

She was in hospital for about five weeks. I visited her twice a day; none of her friends could drive. It entailed two round trips daily of thirty five miles. For a while she did not know whether it was Ash Thursday or Christmas Tuesday. I was beginning to despair. But eventually she began to recover sufficiently to go home. We were on our own her daughter had gone to live with her father. With a little help from a carer to se to her dressing and her toiletries (well someone had to see that she did not dress like Superman, with her knickers on top of her trousers) she slowly started to recover and started to boast, that she was the only one in the family that knew for a fact that she had a brain. Even now after about ten years it still affects her.

lSoon after her being discharged from hospital she realised that she was unlikely to meet another partner through the 'normal' channels. She decided to advertise in the local evening paper "Wanted tall toy boy" Bingo! Along came Eric four years her junior, they had lots in common, and he was six foot two. The most obvious was the fact Christine lived with her 'old fart' of a father and so did Eric. They lived in Clifton Village, after a short courtship they married at Blackpool Register Office and we all went to live at Eric's House in Clifton village. Eric's father who **was** an old fart had bought a small house in the village or I would have not entertained going to live with them. I like to think that I'm not a bad old fart, but he was most definitely he was! It would take up an entire book to go any further into describing that mans traits, so I will waste no further paper on doing so. I will say this that Eric should have been granted a 'Sainthood' for enduring the mans company for as long as he did. Lesser men would have put him down.

Just previous to this I went on a guided tour with the Titan Tour Company to California and the Golden West; this is my journal of it.

The tight Yorkers Journal.

Day One

Up at five am (ungodly and unearthly hour). Titan bus arrived right on the minute. Away to Liverpool, Birkenhead, Stafford, and Birmingham pickups. All on time, then down to oxford for a snack and a pee. Arrived at Heathrow on time, no problems with customs except for my 'Bionic' ankle. Flight took off at 16.45, then it was eleven hours of purgatory (I was full of fart) Legroom negligible , did not sleep a wink. Arrived at Los Angeles bang on time, then another two hours journey to San Diego Pleased to get my head down Lovely room, comfortable bed, big enough for a gang bang, but I've probably forgotten what to do. Travel kettle a boon, coffee maker in the room.

Day Two

Early breakfast then off on a tour of San Diego, with a very informative guide. Tour manager also very pleasant and efficient. San Diego also pleasant and very clean, motorists very considerate (Average thee cars to each family) Toured parks and the zoo and many other points of interest. Too much to be taken in in one day, could spend a fortnight here. Went over a very innovative bridge - middle section moveable to cope with the rush hour's traffic. Across to Colorado a very large military cemetery for the American Navy and Air Force. San Diego is the harbour for American Navy and Air Force, very quiet at the moment. Then back to the old town for lunch. This place seems to be mostly eating and drinking and ice cream parlours. Whether smashing (mid sixties) Petrol $1.11 a gallon. Seem to have teemed up with Crap Welsh Git, Bugger to hell man (Geordie) two Lincolnshire Poachers,

Robin and Lynn, and two Leeds Loaners Blondie and Diana. We all seem to rub together very well. Afternoon we went into the Pacific Whale watching, it was cuck-old..... Bloody cold. did spot one blowing a time or two and caught a **Brief** glimpse of another.

Day Three

Morning call at 6.30then of to Phoenix across arid mountainous country Mountains made of boulders of various sizes . Break at Tacoma 4200ft, windy and cold. Tower started there before the war and finished of by a WW11 Fighter Pilot who went there to find solace and peace and tranquillity. It would have sent me further off my rocker in two days. On to Yucca Crossing. A mixed lot of both desert and arable land. Made arable by canals and irrigation systems, all provided by the Colorado River. Which is used so much that hardly any water flows into the sea? Yucca is practically a desert town, a stopping point for large American trucks which all of them were very smart and clean. Eating very cheap Petrol $1.17 arrived in Phoenix 18.00, did small tour of town had a little snack and went to bed; Video camera doesn't seem to be just right. Put battery on charge hope for the best.

Day Four

Sunday up at 5.30 buffet breakfasts, away at 07.30 across a lot of arid desert little run down communities all over our Town and Country planners would have recurring nightmares. First stop Sedona, red rocks similar to monumental valley. Took some photographs and some camcorder shots. Fine but cold. Around 40 degrees. On to the Grand Canyon (the highlight of my tour) Rose 3000ft in 5 miles around hairpin bends you have to see. -levelled off at 7500 ft temperature 34 degrees. Helicopter ride at 13.30 $85. for half an hour. - very nice , could have been better, we could only fly over the canyon because it was snowing ,in fact we were the last flight that day, two very frightened ladies in the helicopter had to cuddle them, very nice!. Got some very good shots cannot describe Grand Canyon - you have to see it. Then we went to the Imax Theatre- VERY large screen a much better view of the canyon, it had been taken in the summer when the weather was more 'clement, they also showed a white water ride I thought that I was going to get wet.

Away ten to Williams a gentle cowboy town, arrived in a blinding snowstorm at 1800hrs. Temperature 26 degrees that's outside. we were lovely and cosy inside. Hotel very nice, sleeping like a top. better than at home. Lovely meal in nearby restaurant a bit rough but very clean. and a smashing breakfast next morning. Snowed all night. Thought that we were going to be stranded.

Day Five

At least 15 inches of level snow, however the driver put his chains- on and away we went. Only an hour late. Main freeways were closed, had to go on Route 66 arrived, at Kingman at 12.15 another cowboy town went to a supermarket for a meal, everyone very helpful. Had a half a pound hot beef sandwich (lovely) couldn't eat it all. Left at 13.45 for Hoover Dm that's another spectacle. This is a big concrete plug in the Colorado River &600 ft deep. And is colossal, the biggest part of California's electricity is generated there. Then a very fast ride to Las Vegas, arrived at15.30, bedroom like a furnace had to turn the radiators off and go for a stroll round to cool off. Small world. First people that I saw came from Blackpool. Went to a girlie show at night ....Busts more spectacular than talent!! Good trapeze artist. Very good English comedian (Roy Fell) Afterwards we went on a tour to the town and watched a free eight minute laser show in an arcade, it was stunning to say the least. And so to bed knackered.

Day Six

Walked round some of the main casinos went into MGMHotel 5005 bedrooms, front rather ugly. Visited the Golden Nugget, saw the largest nugget in the world worth $1million plus. Found by prospector in Australia apparently by a big slice of fortune. He just kicked it up with his foot. Caesar's palace was the biggest and the best, gaming machines by the thousand. Outside appearance absolutely gi-normous, fountains by the score, the gardens were nice and there were about six people movers (moving paths) in and out. NO windows. Went to imperial Palace to see vintage car show, absolutely tip top, reconditioned /immaculate. Going out tonight to film in the dark. Robin and Lynn have told me to discard the camcorder they will send me a copy of theirs. ...relieved, it was a worry. Discarded teeth they were spoiling my holiday. Temperature today 55ish (should be abut 70) snow forecast for tomorrow.

Day Seven (I think.)

Left Las Vegas 0830. Route 15 for Calico ghost town. Old silver mining community abandoned 1900 ish due to price of silver dropping. Done up recently for the tourist trade. Sheriff immediately arrested tour manager - put in jug - hanging in the morning. Had a shuffle round looked at the entrance of some old mines, had a nice meal. Sheriff threatened to stretch the neck of a young girl on the coach. Real Wild West stuff! On to Bakersfield, nice warm day, mile upon mile or desert and mountains. Wind farms by the thousand! Yes! Mile uoon mile if them. Tour manager said they only provide 2% of California's power, not impressed by their beauty.. They spoilt the scenery. Onto the fruit gardens of California all kinds of fruit and vegetables but especially vines. Arrive at night stop Visalia 1630. Very nice. Hotel best yet.

Day Eight

Up early off to Yosemite Park early-ish snow forecast, may not see it all. Snow chains on again, had a lucky escape. Had to run into a snow drift to avoid crashing. Stuck there for about one and a half hours. On to Yosemite Village, cold and wet a bit disappointing couldn't go to see giant sequoia trees because of snow. However the rest of the glacier (some glazier) valley..... Spectacular! Driver is extremely good, maybe a bit hair rising, adds another thrill to it Arrived at Merson at 18.45. Very tired. Mastered taps and showers at last, (Different in all hotels)

Day Nine

Left Merton at 08.45for San Francisco. Through more fruit farms and wind farms, arrived there at 1200noon, went in over the Oakland double bridge, the one that collapsed in the recent earthquake. Weather nice 65 degrees very lucky no smog-no sign of it. went down to Fisherman's Wharf to look round shops and had a bit of lunch, Clam Chowder and sour bread very nice, then went on a tour of the city with special guide, not very impressed, tout manager had to keep prompting him. It was pointed out that the **Gays** which are in abundance, display a rainbow flag on their property, Arrived at hotel at 16.30, had a rest then went to "Knob Hill" Fairmont Hotel (where the President stays) for buffet dinner, very nice except for raw vegetables. Budweiser $5 a bottle, a few of us were treated to another thrill, going down in the glass escalator in the dark that was fabulous. Then on a night tour of Chinatown. While we there it was the Chinese New Year I saw part of it on the television. Tour manager said all buildings must be one inch apart 'Earthquake regulations' ---didn't seem to be.

Day Ten

Went on 'round the bay' excursion, sailed under Oakland bridge, past Alcatraz (no one ever escaped from there, a good swimmer could have easily have done the distance, but the water is too old to survive The prisoners were not allowed to have cold showers so they cold not acclimatize themselves) Then under the Golden Gate Bridge, lots of very large ugly sea lions were basking in the sun. Had a Fish (?)and chips, worse than poor fish fingers. Then went to my favourite pastime (huh) downtown shopping at Macys. Very large departmental store seven stories and a restaurant. Shopping not cheap in this city. Petrol $1, 35. Rode down in cable car. Figured out how they work, 'being pondering all my life' not telling you, will have to work it out by yourself. Getting back on a Saturday afternoon meant 'shanks pony' up those very steep hills made me puff a bit. Saw something very unusual, a man with a cat on a lead begging. It is Chinese New Years celebrations tonight a quarter of a million are expected to watch it…. temperature must be about 70 degrees in the shade. Going out to night to local pub with the Crap Welsh Git and the two Leeds lasses and the Bugger to hell man. Substitute 'pub' for Crap …what a dive! Sawdust floor! 150 decibel 'music' Pleased when Al Capone didn't come in. Went to a Chinese Cafe for a 'nuclear' meal

(Fission chips) very god.

Day Eleven

Up at 0700. Rotten breakfast (what day is it) away at 08.30 Went past the, 'little boxes on the hillside' the song illustrates it very well. Looking back could see the fog swelling round the bay, we had been very lucky. Nice drive own to Monterey saw our first policemen there three of them on motor bikes. Went to discount market, clothes quite cheap there. Had a snack, and then went on his famous 17 mike drive. Housing round here costs millions. Famous golf courses and links. Someone said links have no trees?? We saw several grazing deer, cheapest golf round $ 175 dearest at Pebble Beach $225 a round. No walking down the fairways, special paths for electric buggies. Seat up to six. Pebble Beach was Bing Crosby's favourite club. Next stop was Dirty Harrys where Clint Eastwood was Mayor very nice, could have stayed there a bit longer. Bags of Art Galleries and salons, also the smelliest toilets that we have seen. someone should tell Dirty Harry. Also very few dogs, no dog shit. , and no litter. Then on to the Big Sur, giant redwoods, extra large tale poles, stopped at several places for us to take photographs, it was a coastal ride, and at San Lucia saw at least five whales, plus several rocks which kidded us. After another exhilarating ride of at least fifty cliff hangers and an equal number of hairpin bends arrived at St Simeon at about 18.15 went into Jacuzzi for half an hour, felt very refreshed. Swollen ankle went down. Had a good dinner ant went to bed knackered, WR Hearst (Patry Hearst's father) lived here in his palatial palace a very luxurious place. Would liked to have visit it, bur time didn't allow.

Day Twevle

08.00 departure for a long ride 270 miles first stop Danish town of Solvang. Danish parties a speciality, nice clean town. Met a woman shopkeeper there from my home town of Barnsley, could tell by her dialect, had quite a nice chat with her. Then on to Santa Barbara, looking a bit gloomy there but warm enough had a nuclear meal on the wooden pier. Very nice acrobatic birds cadging chips, supposed to be a lot of pelicans there, saw one. Plenty of oil rigs on the sea horizon. Rain al the way down to Los Angeles very tiring journey arrived at 07.00 (nicest hotel yet) went into he Jacuzzi for an hour, very hot very good. Went into the pool, forgotten how to swim. Scared to take my feet off the bottom. Supper in hotel nice very expensive. ... And so to bed.

Data Thirteen

Went to Hollywood to universal studios, poor day, and cold. But no rain. Would have enjoyed it had it been warmer. Also cold aluminium seating did not help.. Rejuvenated in Jacuzzi.

Day Fourteen

Disney land today , ideal weather , just right about 70 degrees. Cajoled to go on all those hair-raising rides, enjoyed it really, not as bad as cork screwing in a Lancaster Bomber (was a bit younger and sillier then) highlight for me was the circular screen cinema show … Fantastic! Caught a bit of sun on my face today, ventured out of hotel for a change, enjoyed it, had a nice meal. Had a T bone steak and all the trimmings. $9/95 that was cheap but excellent.

Day Fifteen

We went for a walk in the morning, very warm in deed. Up in the 80's would have gone into the pool but the trunks would not be dry to pack way for the home flight, had twenty winks longer in bed. Left hotel at 12,30 for tour of the Sunset Strip, Chinese Theatre, Stars Footprints and Mexican Market (high quality leather and fancy goods) wish we could have stayed here a bit longer. Crap welsh git won the competition for guessing the total mileage of the tour jammy sod 2887 (?) I thought it was more. Forward to the Airport and goodbyes to our excellent tour manager could not say any thing about her than excellent. Boring two hrs waiting to fly had a cup of tea (?) witch pee better disribes it. Flew at 10.30pm, very uneventful flight fared better than the flight here, still couldn't sleep. Arrived Heathrow at 1600, through customs straight onto Titan bus and did a reversal of the journey down. 5 hours later arrived home at 22.30 didn't feel too bad guess what, a teapot full of lovely real tea

If I have missed owt out HARD CHEDDAR.

At this time I was seventy four, going on twenty four I did kinds of foolish things, like going up on the roof to put two new chimney pots on and various mad things. The house at Clifton was not clean. It needed bottoming, two very untidy men had lived in it for years and it was very tired, I took out the fire place in the lounge and put a new one in. And had a gas fire installed. There had been an electric fire in the dining room but Eric's father had taken it, to my delight. There was no hole there for a fire to be fitted so I had to make one. There was a chimney but the fireplace had been bricked up. So I had to draw on my reserves to Britches Arse Steam and good old dose of Percy Variance' came in handy once more. I then constructed a wooden surround and tiled inside it and made a hearth with two breeze blocks and tiled that then I had a gas fire installed. These two gas fires provided a blessing because we had several power cuts. I was in my elements for a while. it kept me out of that mischief that I have mislaid.

After this I started to get a bit bored with myself. You see Clifton village is well placed in beautiful countryside, but it is absolutely devoid of any social activities, there is no pub nor any meeting place what so ever. No Church or Chapel or pub, and all work and no play made George a dull boy. So I used to visit my daughter Sandra in Youlgrave Derbyshire frequently. Sandra and George were the tenants of a very busy pub there, I used to enjoy going, because I could help both in the kitchen and the pub. They do not keep the pub the pub keeps them. Also they employ a large number of local staff.

Because of the considerable time that I was spending there, some friends of mine, Andy and John, both employed at the pub, suggested that I should apply for a council bungalow in the village, I said because I was not local I would not stand much chance of getting one. A while later my circumstances changed due to the fact that I had a stroke. And lost a lot of the sight in my right eye. The lads did not like me driving all the way down here so they used to fetch me and bring me home a150 mile round journey. While visiting I eventually did apply for a bungalow, by a few exaggerations of the truth, only small ones of course (I only tell lies when the truth won't answer he same purpose).A bungalow was offered me at the top end of the village it needed redecorating. Andy and Gillian, with a bit of help from Sandra, soon licked into shape. So once more I up sticks and went to be a Pommie, that the name for Yougrave villagers.

A few weeks later the council decided to rewire it, typical isn't it? That was an awful experience, like living in a building site. My electrician grand-son-in-law told me that in his opinion that it did not want rewiring. All it needed was some extra sockets and a new consumer unit. The existing wire was up to date. When examining the new and the old they were identical. I had very good relations with my neighbours; the big snag living there was that I had to go up a flight of steps to get to it. This did not help my Rheumatism and all my other I's'm's. Not long after this another bungalow came empty I applied for it the housing manager said that I didn't qualify for it because I had not been a tenant long enough. I asked him what the qualifying period was he said twelve months; I told him if that was the case I did qualify I had been there twelve months and a day. , after furbishing the requisite medical information about the state of my health including my lung problems from my doctor. The bungalow was allocated to me. It was simply, but nicely decorated, you see the previous tenants only lived there a month the lady could not settle, they had lived in a big house and she felt claustrophobic. They had a new kitchen fitted and had it re-carpeted throughout, all the doors had been replaced, it must have cost a small fortune. As they took all the carpets with them I had to replace them. I lived there for four years.

Socially Youlgrave is a model village , almost all the houses are old , but I can assure you , they are modern inside, it is busy as Clifton is quiet, there is a Church ant two Chapels. Three pubs and a British Legion. And reading room and a Village Hall where annually the locals put on a pantomime, this production puts into shade many professional shows; it goes on for a fortnight. And is usually booked throughout. There is also a tennis club, a bowling club. The green is a credit to someone. A cricket club with its own pavilion. And a football ground. We have our own medical centre complete with its own dispensary. The bus service is also very good.

My pride and joy at Youlgrave

There were five shops when I first started to visit You grave, two have since closed. Also there was "chip oil", that had to close because of the owners over familiarity with three legged horses, that he indulged, in other words, he backed too many losers. Peak park planners would not let it open again because of the car parking regulations.

While I was there I stared to make pork pies for the pub, mostly they were for hatching, matching, and dispatching celebrations. I made them to a recipe which I got from his Yorkshire Post newspaper in 1978 to which I added my own secret ingredients. Apparently they were well received because several people asked me to make one for them. I soon started to make them on a fairly regular basis. The chef, the aforementioned Andy at the pub said I should enter competitions with them, but I didn't pursue that line. But I did make a lot. I was a bit soft, I could not refuse anyone. One Christmas I made forty of them, these by the way were not individual pies. They were full loaf tin size. I did not give them away I charged the going rate of two pounds a pound for them. It was something that I enjoyed doing every year at the prize giving of the Domino competitions I made individual pies for about thirty. These were eaten with mushy peas. It was a lot more demanding to make these, because I did not have a professional die.

You grave is one of the most popular Well Dressing villages. The tradition goes back donkeys years probably to pagan times. For the unenlightened. On first day the proceeding (there are five wells) the local Vicar blesses each well individually. Well Dressing is a fine art. Each well is designed by a different person. They are made from local flower and fauna. They are set in special clay fitted in wooden trays mounted on a wooden frame about five feet by eight foot. The frames and the clay are immersed in the local river for a week before working on. Each well depicts a different Biblical Scene. It takes all week to complete it. Often all this is done behind closed doors. However some will welcome visitors to come and watch. -the best way to see how it is done. They are on display a week sadly if the weather is hot the clay shrinks, and the display deteriorates badly by the end of the week. Coaches full of people come from near and far to view these visions of loveliness, there is also a lot of quaffing of ale in the local drinking clinics during the displays.

Also at Youlgrave we used to have a Carnival unfortunately it is no longer held. The reason being was because toe elderly ladies were the organizers, and they discouraged anyone else from interfering with the arrangements. Consequently when they decided to retire, no one else had the expertise as to how to go about things. I think also, that insurance came into the equation. It is a great shame; these traditions are the life and soul of village life.

On one carnival day I donned mi sen up as Charlie Chaplin. And whilst assembling in the field waiting to be judged, a very near acquaintance of mine approached me and we were engrossed in conversation for quite a while. Later that evening in the pub overheard him saying, who was that chap that was dressed as Charlie Chaplin. He could not believe that it was *himself*. We had a good laugh about it.

I may as well blow the trumpet about my daughter's pub. The George Hotel. It is a cosy well kept place with a wide and varied menu. They are well patronised, also they have won their Breweries best decorated pub prize quite a number of times.

The George Hotel, Youlgreave

Me at the carnival

Whilst living in Derbyshire I did a bit more globe trotting. I went across the pond again to America, to the east coast this time to New York. I was totally unimpressed by JFK airport. nowt near as good as Ringway. We spent two days in New York sight seeing, the highlights being the Statue of Liberty, Ellis Island, Rockefeller buildings , Greenwich Village and several other places. My travelling partner was very unadventurous, especially for a young 'UN (early thirties) I wanted to go up the Empire Building, but he was afraid of heights so we did not go.

Then we started our coach tour, our first port of call was Boston, where we of coarse had to go to the Boston Tea Party younger ones will have to fetch their history books out to look that one up. We also visited a very large fruit and vegetable market, where I had some Clam chowder and sour bread, it was delicious, and I can almost taste it now.

On to our next destination that was Quebec; we stopped quite often to view the wonderful colours of the September Fall. In Quebec we saw the heights of Abraham which General Wolfe had to scale to conquer the city we also saw a spectacular water fall, there was a bridge over it but ny companion would not put a foot on it, Its a good job he was' born in the twenties or we would have all be sporting swastikas' on our lapels.

The next place was the Canadian capital. Ottawa I recall the tour guide saying that they were only two seasons in Ottawa, Winter and road digging, we got the drift, they were digging left right and centre all the time we were there.

Montreal was our next stop, there we went to see the site if the Olympic games, plus several other highlights. The stadium is still open but every thing is deteriorating due to lack of maintenance Memories are funny things aren't they? I a remember things from donkey years ago, but recent things allude me. I do recall that there were as much development going on underground as there was at street level. they say that there is more underground shopping, as there is at steet level, you would think that Canada was short of space. Had to tell my friend that if he did not alter his ways he could go his way and I would go mine. He did try a bit harder after that.

The next call was Toronto, the Jewel of Canada. It is a lovely modern city the highlight of which is the CN, tower until recently was the tallest free standing building in the world ,(I think that honour is now held in Kabala Lumpa) there is a revolving restaurant on the top. Wild horses would not have stopped me from going up the CN tower, I had a meal in the restaurant and during the meal it revolved full circle. Which was extremely fortunate for me? I had placed my camcorder on the window ledge beside me, not taking into consideration that the restaurant was stationary and the window ledge was revolving, it came back to me an hour tater, I had another big stoke of luck that evening, at the base of the Tower is the world's first Sky dome. The dome was retractable and there was a game taking place at the time. I was able to video it, through the glass floor of the tower of course the players looked like midgets. While I was in Toronto I tried to make contact with Barry Watts who was the Bomb Aimer in my crew during my excursions in the war. He was from Toronto, however the quest did not bear ant fruit, the receptionist at the hotel was very good, and she tried her best to no avail.

On now to the highlight of the tour, first of all we called at the manicured village of Niagara on the Lake. On the southern edge if Lake Ontario. This is the prettiest village that I have ever seen. A festival began there in 1962 as a theatrical memorial to George Bernard Shaw. The place was absolutely awash with hanging baskets and flower beds, there was also a big statue of the man.

Our next stop was the Niagara Falls which was the highlight of the tour. where the hell does all the water come from.? I had to persuade my friend to go on the Maid of the mist. (It was hard work) we were almost taken under the falls, we had plastic Macs on otherwise we would have been drenched with he spray. The immediate surroundings were beautifully laid out with flower beds. But the town itself did not impress me. It looked tatty, and the hotel was bloody horrible. Then we went back through customs into the states.

The next stop was to be a visit it a Hamish farm. It was like stepping back in time. That was very enlightening and they laid on an excellent meal which is more than could be said about Canadian meals, my accountant had told me about the poor meals he had in Canada he was right.

The next stop was Washington DC where our highlight was the Air and Space Museum; there was a replica of the space ship that was used to go to the moon. I could see why a lot of people are sceptical about this happening, as it looked like some schoolboy had made it, with the help of Fred Cano that they had been cobbled together. We saw replicas of every kind of air memorabilia you can imagine we saw the actual plane that Lindberg first flew the Atlantic, could have spent days there. My companion sat on the steps smoking. But I did persuade him to go to the Natural History Museum which was another good experience, quite impressive. we saw many other things including The Capital Building, which is very striking, We did not see much of the White House because Nelson Mandela was visiting that day, so the place was swarming with security. Next we saw the statues of George Washington, and Abraham Lincoln. And the JFK museum where all the flags of the United Nations are displayed. Then on to Arlington Cemetery where JFK and his wife are buried, the eternal flame honours their passing. Washington is a well laid out clan city. Building is only allowed up to fourteen storeys, but apparently they have a very big crime rate we were perused by several beggars, mostly unkempt young men.

Philadelphia was our next port of call. This was just for us to be fed and watered. We did get to see the famous Liberty Bell which is badly cracked. Time did not allow us to explore any further. Then on to New York. We had to pass through Harlem, where you get a prize if you spot a white man. . The next stop was to be JFK airport. When we were getting off the bus the driver put his hand to for remuneration. I shook it vigorously well surly he wasn't expecting a tip. Goodness me it was the first time he on the whole journey that he even proffered his hand. He sure as heck hadn't offered a hand in assistance to carry any luggage for me, or even steady me when I was getting off the coach with a stick in one hand and a small case in the other. Any how it had been a good holiday. Then it was time to cross the pond and home

Then I got the urge to on a cruise on the med, staring and finishing at the beautiful city of Venice. After a flight from Heathrow we were met at the airport and taken straight to the cruise ship, and we were off very soon. After nights cruising the first port of call was Olympia in Greece, where the Olympic Games were first held. Several earthquakes have long devastated the place. It was obviously an extensive site that has been well tidied up. Our guide had the usual nine league legs on, so I had to sprint to keep up with him, he was very good at pointing out the salient points, it was very interesting, also it was very cold , frosty in fact, most of us had thin clothes on.

For the evening dress I wore my blazer with the RAF insignia on, the krauts did not appreciate it, but the Dutch people really showed their appreciation. Especially one of the ladies who came up and kissed me and thanked me profusely for what the RAF had done for them at the end of WW11 that's when the RAF took food to a starving populace. Each time we met she made a fuss of me and thanked me again, I think if I had played my cards right I might have clicked.

Then on to Alexandria, that was the filthiest place I have seen. The main streets were not so bad, but the side streets were dirty and absolutely awash with rubbish. Many of the older buildings were in a decrepit state. I think (god forbid it) that if there is another earthquake there many of them would collapse. The main tourist areas were nice and clean, but I only ate on the cruise ship, (one deli belly is enough) we went by coach to Cairo; I was shocked to discover that between Cairo and Alexandria, it is essential to drive in convoy protected by armed guards. This is because of the large number of Bandits in the region. Cairo has improved a bit since my first visit, but still very squalid in places. It is still worth a visit. Our first meal stop was at the manor house where Churchill and Roosevelt met during the war. Was the last to get off the coach and my arthritis did not like the long flight of stairs I had to scale on the way to the restaurant. So by the time I reached the buffet table it had been attacked by the greedy Yanks who had loaded their plates up (as usual they left half to it uneaten) I loudly voiced my opinion about them. But it was like water of a ducks back. When I reached the desert section, it was the same story... why should I expect any different. We also went to the Pyramids, where we saw loads of begging children, quite persistent they were, also the Sphinx where the surroundings had been excavated to expose many more things. We also had a brief visit to the Cairo museum where it was so busy that I saw almost nothing. I was amazed at how many Oriental people we saw, I can not recall seeing so many on my previous visit. Cairo is not as dirty as Alexandria but they are working on it. Back in convoy to the cruise ship where we had a decent meal. The greedy Yanks couldn't grab all the food. One of them came to me afterwards and apologised about the behaviour of some of his countrymen. He also said he was disgusted by their behaviour.

Next day we should have visited Port Said. But because of the political situation there we could not go. The next port of call was the Island of Rhodes, where it was very cold, I enjoyed the coach ride, but not much else there was too much walking, once more the guide had his nine league boots on, is it an endemic disease with guide?, I have never enjoyed being tail end Charlie, but I had to get on with it. The next place that we visited was near Athens, where the harbour was littered with rusty hulks of ships, I think they must have been scuttled during the war and re-floated.

The highlight there was the Acropolis, but I was strongly advised not to go because of the walking and the steps that were involved. It was a cold and miserable and not much to do, so I went back to the liner where it was nice and warm. We then called at Phyla's (may have spelled this incorrectly) It was pretty abysmal, dismal and gloomy; I didn't find much to write home about.

The next place that we should have visited was the Corinth Canal. This would have been the highlight of the cruise for me. For some unexplained reason this did not happen no explanation was given. We then were almost becalmed, I could have paddled faster, and apparently we were killing time so that we could dock at the allocated time in Venice. The consensus of opinion, voiced by the well seasoned passengers was that the cruise had been well under par, I was a little disappointed but worse things have happened to me.

I got really settled in the bungalow, I had a six foot by twelve foot greenhouse and the appropriate cold frames. I only grew tomatoes and flowers, all from seed and a few cuttings which I acquired by devious means. With coming from a gardening family I knew a thing or two on this subject.

My garden was not very big. The local council cut the grass for us. I had two small flower beds. And I bedecked the front with hanging baskets, flower pots and troughs. I was chuuffed when I got a commendation from the local council for my efforts in my first year there. We were well looked after by a warden called Jackie. She was very affable; nothing was too much trouble for her.

Every year a flower and garden produce show was held in the Village Institute the local Allotment Association do the organisation. They received good and varied entries, fruit and vegetables, with classes for jam and cakes, plants, photography, artistry, even scarecrows, plus a children's section.

One year I had several entries and did quite well, my daughter at the pub also had some entries and between us we got six prizes, I overheard someone saying , 'Bloody comer's in, winning all these prizes' It was said loudly within my earshot and was only a joke.

I must include this memory while I am talking about garden shows. My granddad was going by train to Southport flower show in a side-corridor train. The chap alone in the next compartment was snoring his head off. Granddad crept in to him and during one of his heavy inhalations; he popped a three pence size coin piece of snuff under his hooter and swiftly departed to his own compartment. Granddad said that the poor chap had not got a clue what had happened to him, and there was blood and snot all over the compartment. He nearly did the nine things recited by Mr Bishop in an earlier chapter.

It must be something in the Parkinson blood line. But the next memory concerns 'blind dates' Christine always brags that she must be the only person she knows who has had a 'blind date' in a hospital bed, Maybe I am the only elderly chap who has had a 'blind date' on a cruise ship. I fancied going to the Norwegian Fjords. Some 'excursions' of my youth. Were up in the airspace over Norway, in the region where the Tirpitz was sunk. To cut expenses I told the cruise company that I would share a cabin rather than pay the extortionate single cabin supplement.

My cabin companion turned out to be a twenty four carat gentleman. A great chap called Mr Frank Vickers, a Norse name if there ever was one! From Cleethorpes. I could not have wished for a better shipmate. We hit it off immediately, quite a lot of our fellow travellers thought that we were brothers. We did not live in each' pockets and that suited us both. This cruise was the best. We did not have any need to grumble about anything whatsoever. The weather was brilliant throughout. Ninety five per cent of the time the sea was like a mill pond. The temperature was in the seventies even at North Cape. This is where it never goes dark in summer even at one o'clock in the morning you could see to read a newspaper. The air up there is so fresh it is intoxicating. And the coffee was so dear I asked if I could take out a mortgage to pay for it.

We sailed from Harwich to Olden end called at several places on the way up the coast, up to the Artic Circle where it was announced that as we were approaching, the Arctic Circle and we should all get ready to jump over it. Then up to the North Cape where we only had a few hours, I could have easily spent a couple of days there and not see it all. However, we could not have afforded it, two coffees cost the equivalent of fifteen ponds sterling. Then back down the coast visiting different places, to Bergen and thence back to Blighty. The consensus of opinion about this cruise was that was one hundred per cent top rate. His food and the entertainment and crew were excellent, food was served from seven o'clock in the morning until eleven at night, our friends from over the pond would have been in paradise.

Unfortunately my health started to deteriorate I had another little stroke and was taken to Callow hospital in Chesterfield where they told me that my arteries were clogged up and needed scraping out or I may lose the sight of my other eye. This was done at the end of October in Northern General Hospital in Sheffield. After the operation I was discharged too soon and did not pick up as I should, when I had to go to hospital with bowel trouble. I deteriorated further and just before Christmas I had a bad attack of bronchitis, (which I thought was Pneumonia) which set me back still further. My daughter and her husband Eric were visiting Youlgrave for Christmas, so they were able to keep an eye on me, I would have been in a mess without them. As I felt that I was deteriorating badly, I asked them if I could return with them to Clifton for a while until I recovered. They agreed to that, but things got worse, I had to have several visits from a local doctor plus a couple of visits from the emergency doctor. Then I had a heart attack and had to go in Preston Royal Infirmary. That was prolonged by a severe bout of diarrhoea which really set me back. After a while I knew that I was not going to look after myself. It was decided that I should stay with them. For a while, my state of health was up and down I was too weak to climb the stairs and had to sleep downstairs. That was not practical so I had a stair lift fitted, which solved that particular problem. ! (If everything was so easy?) In March I had another mild heart attack and was hospitalised again. After a day or two I was transferred to a ward that was rampant with the Norfolk Virus, (sick and diarrhoea, to thee and me) of course I got my fair share and was really ill for four days. I was put in a side room; cleanliness was a foreign word while I was there. My toilet was left in an uncleaned state for several days. The hygiene of both doctors and nurses left a lot to be desired because the staffs was so busy, we did not get the attention we deserved

Granby House opened by HRH The Prince Of Wales and HRH Princess Diana. On the 9/3/90, it was then in the Abbeyfield Association. It was taken over by local trustees on the 12/02/05.

Then I started to recover Christine kept a close eye on me making sure that didn't do too many silly things, Several lady carers came to see to my hygiene needs. (Never in the field of human caring, have I been looked after by so many for such a long time.... 'With apologies to good old Winston Spencer Churchill' I must say I have little complain about regarding Social Services.

Unfortunately relations started to deteriorate with my relations, (thes are too painful to put on paper) it will have to suffice that we fell out on the Saturday evening and by the Monday afternoon they had put me in a home. The home was at Marton few miles away. It was a lovely purpose built place about thirty residents of which I could only converse with one all he others had varying stages if dementia. The staff were wonderful with me.

Fortunately my daughter at Youlgrave got to know what happened and by a big stroke of luck told me that there was an empty room at Granby House Youlgrave (formally Abbeyfield) and she had inquired if I could come there, the answer was in the affirmative and I grabbed it with both hands. This pace is what is called a Very Sheltered Home, it t may not be the best, it's better than that. It should have a medal of Pure Gold the size of a bucket end. It is absolutely the tops it is only a small place, eight bedrooms, a nicely appointed Kitchen a lovely dinning room and a large conservatory, and a very nice bath and shower room. It is run by local people who are the trustees, the Secretary is Pat Cleaver and is subsidised by the Local Council. The resident housekeeper is Anne Bullimore; she is assisted by Margaret Bird and two other cleaning ladies. Margaret acts as house keeper when Anne has her days off, also a young lady called Lenca, helps out as House keeper- cleaner, when they are both having a day off or a holiday. This is heaven, it's clean and warm and the meals are excellent, a decent varied diet. We have to provide our own breakfast and supper. The bathing commodities are unsurpassed, a lot of the rooms are en-suite we have a laundry room, also a subsidised Laundry where we can send our laundry, once a fortnight. We have a Whist Drive once a fortnight and have an outing at least once a month. Some times I think I have died a gone to heaven. I think that I have adequately told you about the village in a previous chapter, but the one that stands out is the village medical centre, it literally677 is just across the road and they are quire wonderful, especially when compared to some others. Of coarse I have had to test the waters of the local hospitals while I have been here, a time or two, that chap up there occasionally shouts for me to come in, I shout back. Bugger off I am not ready just yet. I have an ambition; I would like to get to the upper place for a fortnight, before the devil gets to know. By the way the Carnival has restarted and it is a resounding success.

Now this I must tell you, this is bang up to date. Recently was the occasion to the century here. The two of our eldest residents tied the knot, Mr Eric Rome who us pushing ninety six and Sheila Mather whose ninety two next week. They have been living 'over the brush' for three years and decided to make it decent. I don't think that it was a shot gun affair, well, time will tell. It was magnificent, they only decided to get married two weeks ago, and everything was perfect. They married at Hassop Hall and we were all invited, the weather was perfect the meal was a real treat. Could not have done better me sen!!!. Everything was perfect and the wine and the champagne, flowed quite freely. I sang a love song advise for Sheila, (Keep young and beautiful) I would have liked to sing to Eric (please release let meet me go) but I don't know him that well so restrained myself. They have been featured in television and the radio and in a lot of newspapers quite celebrities they are, like I said previously. You can learn old dog's new tricks.

Well I am coming to the end of my tissue of tales, I hope that you have been able to understand some of it, I cannot pretend to be able to express myself as much as I would liked, and the grammar, well I did burn the school down when I was quite young, so what the hell do you expect.

Apart from only having one eye, a squint, and a pain in the neck (I can not spell the fancy name for that) Angina, and a dickie ticker, pneumoconiosis, Chronic Bronchitis plus Arthritic thighs knees and shoulders A bionic ankle, ingrown toe nails, I am in pretty good shape for a young 'un

Like have said before. I am a lot better than was before I started being as bad as I had been, that's apart from being Knackered

My financial position is very similar, I am a rich man I have enough money to last me the rest of my life. That's provided I shuffle off this motel coil tomorrow. In the mean time I am just getting on with it.

I do realise that my story is a bit disjointed in places trouble is, so am I.

Just one thought has crossed my Brain?? Shortly after WW2 the Lion Oil Company in Alberta Canada offered me a job. What if ??